"LITTLE" Thoughts FOR THE Day

"LITTLE" Thoughts FOR THE Day

Encouraging Daily Thoughts for Administrators and Teachers to Share with Their Students

JOYCE O'BRYANT

NASHVILLE

NEW YORK • LONDON • MELBOURNE • VANCOUVER

"LITTLE" Thoughts FOR THE Day

Encouraging Daily Thoughts for Administrators and Teachers to Share with Their Students

Published in New York, New York, by Morgan James Publishing. Morgan James is a trademark of Morgan James, LLC. www.MorganJamesPublishing.com

The Morgan James Speakers Group can bring authors to your live event. For more information or to book an event visit The Morgan James Speakers Group at www.TheMorganJamesSpeakersGroup.com.

ISBN 978-1-68350-805-2 paperback
ISBN 978-1-68350-806-9 eBook
Library of Congress Control Number: 2017915896

Cover Design by:
Rachel Lopez
www.r2cdesign.com

Interior Design by:
Bonnie Bushman
The Whole Caboodle Graphic Design

For all those students, both young, and young adults,
who have had such an impact on my life.

TABLE OF CONTENTS

(Because this book cannot be formatted according to the current calendar year, it follows the number of school days, in each month accordingly)

INTRODUCTION

This book came about after I worked as a principal in a private Christian elementary school. Every morning I would greet the students over the intercom and pray for their day. As time went on, I decided to share a Thought for the Day with them before prayer. This book is the result of those Thoughts shared daily with those students to encourage and motivate them.

We often have no idea what some children experience on a daily basis. I was amazed at how much these Thoughts meant to my students, as they often referred to something that we had discussed which they had been dealing with.

Whether this book is used by administrators, teachers, or parents, its purpose is that it be used to inspire and encourage elementary students daily. It has been written as a Christian book, but it can be used by any of those working with young children.

This book has been written in a simplistic manner to connect with pre-school thru 5th graders, primarily. It has been formatted according to the school year, and significant holidays are included to make the Thoughts significant to students during those times.

Parents may find this book beneficial also, as a way to encourage and brighten their child's day as they head off to school daily. We love our children—we need to encourage them!

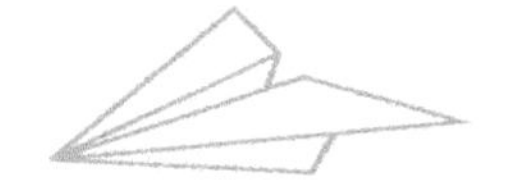

SEPTEMBER

Day 1

"I will treat others the way I want them to treat me."

Think about that statement. How do you want to be treated? Do you want people to be ugly to you? Do you want them to accuse you of doing things you didn't do? Do you want them to talk about you behind your back? Of course not. I bet you want others to be kind to you, to be fair with you, and to just treat you in a respectful way. That's what we all want.

Well, if you want others to treat you this way, why shouldn't you treat others the same way? Before you do something that you are not sure of—ask yourself—"Would I want my parents, my friends, my teachers, or anyone else I know to treat me this way?" If the answer is no, then change your behavior. You'll be glad you did.

Our actions speak louder than the words we say. Kind actions bring warm feelings that can never be repaid. We should always stop and ask, how do I want to be treated? Then act that way toward others to show that God's word we have heeded (Author Unknown).

Dear God,

Thank You for this first day of school. We pray for a good day today. We pray that today, as we are starting a new school year, that we will stop and think about the way we are treating those around us. Help us to treat others kindly; the way You want us to treat them.

Day 2

"In happy moments, praise God."

As you start a new school year, the smiles on your faces show that you are excited to see your friends and teachers. You will have lots of happy moments each and everyday as you talk with those who are so close to you.

Go into your classroom this year excited to be with those you missed over the summer. Praise God for them as you smile, for He is the one who has brought all of you together.

When we are having those happy moments, we need to stop and praise the One who gives them to us—God. When you do that, God is having a happy moment as well. He is smiling down on you.

Our prayer is that you will have lots of happy moments this new school year. Praise God for them!

Dear God,

Help us remember to give You praise throughout our day. Thank You for giving us those happy moments and help us be grateful for all You give us daily.

Day 3

"Each day offers a new start to do my best, as the Lord would have it."

This Thought for the Day basically means that if you have messed up and not done as well in your behavior, or in the way you have been treating others this week, you have a chance to start fresh today and make this day the best it can be. When we have done things that are not pleasing to God, He forgives us when we ask Him to.

Imagine the whiteboard in your classroom and how easily your teacher erases marks that are on it. The same is true when we mess up with God. He erases those "mess-ups" and our slate is clean again. Isn't that a wonderful thought? We do nothing to deserve this from Him, but He loves us so much that He is willing to wipe our sins away when we ask Him to.

We have a chance to start all over with each new day and make it the best we can make it. So let's make this day the best it can be and please the Lord.

Dear God,

Thank You for this good first week of school. We pray that each of us will start fresh today and do exactly what is asked of us. Help us to remember that You forgive us of those things we do wrong and that You are our strength to start fresh each new day.

Day 4

"How I look is not nearly as important as how I act."

As we all dress for the day, we take a lot of time deciding what we will be wearing. Girls look lovely in their beautiful dresses, skirts, and pants. Boys are so handsome in their colorful pullover shirts, matching pants, and ties (when they choose to wear them). Everyone works very hard to look great everyday. How we look is very important to all of us.

However, if you are acting in a way that is not pleasing to the Lord, ***that*** is going to stand out to everyone, to the point that no one is going to see all those nice things you are wearing. ***Your behavior*** is going to take everyone's attention.

Remember to act as nicely as you look. We call that being beautiful and handsome on the inside ***and*** outside.

Dear God,

Help us remember that how we act all the time is so much more important than how we look. Appropriate actions make us look even better. Help us to be good examples for You today and to be beautiful and handsome on the inside, as well as the outside.

Day 5

"Always remember that you are unique—just like everyone else."

What does unique mean? It means being the only one of its kind. So when we say that you are unique—it means that there is no one else like you. God made you special—there's only one you.

Everybody is different or unique. What a person looks like on the outside has nothing to do with what is inside. Every person has special talents and special qualities given to them by God.

Listen to this short poem: *Everyone is unique, Special in their own way, They talk, walk, work, and play, Differently each and everyday, The only thing that's the same, About two people side by side, Is that both were made by God, And with both, He will abide (Author Unknown).*

Dear God,

Thank You for making each of us so special and unique. We know that You have a plan for each and every person on this earth. Help us to use our unique abilities to honor You and to fulfill the plan that You have for us here on earth.

Day 6

"When I start something, I finish it."

Have you ever seen someone start to do something and then they get caught up in doing something else and never complete the first thing they started? It is very important to complete what we start.

Think about it, if you are in your class and your teacher gives you two worksheets to do and you do a little bit on the first one and then go on to the second one, but never go back to the first one—you probably are not going to make a very good grade.

It is very important that you finish what you start. Whether it be your schoolwork, your chores around the house, helping your teacher, or whatever you start to do—you should always finish what you start.

You may have to remind yourself to stay with a task all the way to the end, but it's worth the reminder to keep yourself focused on what you need to finish.

Get in a habit of staying with what you start and don't go on to anything else until you finish the first thing. This is an important lesson to learn in life. You will always have things you have to do, but stay with one thing until it's finished and then go to the next.

The sooner you learn to do this, the better off you will be. Remember: When you start something, finish it! Things will go better for you if you do.

Dear God,

Help us to stay focused on the tasks ahead of us and to work hard to complete the things we have to do before going on to something else.

Day 7

"Everyday is the first day of the rest of my life."

This thought for the day came from a man named L. Vincent Majestic. It is a very powerful statement with lots of meaning behind it.

Think about that. We get up everyday with a brand new day ahead of us, and we can look at it as a brand new start. That's great, isn't it?

It doesn't matter how much we may have messed up the day before because we know the Lord forgives us if we ask Him to. So we can look at each day we have been blessed with as a fresh beginning. A chance to do better.

We should cherish everyday of our lives and look forward to a better, brighter day. Today will not be perfect, but we can make today a day to enjoy.

We have the opportunity everyday to make each new day the best it can be. We have a choice everyday to make this day better than the one before. A fresh start. The first day of the rest of our lives.

Dear God,

Thank You for fresh starts. Help us to always strive to do better and better and to live a life You are pleased with. Help us to rely upon You daily for guidance and direction.

Help us to start fresh each day and forgive us when we don't get it right.

Day 8

"When spider webs unite, they can tie up a lion."

This Thought for the Day is an Ethiopian proverb with such a great meaning. You know that one spider web by itself is not such a strong thing. We may not like them, and we may be scared of seeing the spider that made it, but they are fairly easy to break through. However, lots of spider webs together are much stronger. And according to this proverb, they can tie up a lion. That's strong, isn't it?

It means that when many weaker things (like people) work together or unite, they can be strong enough to do great things (like the spider webs tying up the lion).

If each of us makes a little effort, we can achieve great things by working together. Don't ever think you are too small to make a difference. If you are working with other people, you can make a big difference. This is important.

If you are working with God at the center of what you are doing, you can do more than you ever imagined. He will see to that.

Simply put, small things can combine to form a big thing. The power of one is small, but the power of many, working together, is mighty.

Think about it, if all of your class works together to do something, you can accomplish a lot. Keep up the good work. Work together to do great things—capture that imaginary lion!

Dear God,

Help us to remember today that if we work hard and work together, we can do so much more than working only on our own. Help us to be team players—those who want to pitch in and support and encourage others. Help us to look for opportunities to help others and to do our part.

Day 9

"I will be the best me I can be. I will not be satisfied with a 'so-so' me. I want to learn more each day, set goals and reach new ones each day of my life."

The author of the above Thought for the Day is unknown, but he or she definitely had the right idea when they made the statement. There are many people in the history of our country who have continued to set goals for themselves, who have believed in themselves, and who have done great things because of this attitude.

When we think about these people who refused to give up and who continued to set new goals for themselves and reach them, it is good to look at the difference between a super ball and a raw egg.

A super ball is one of those very hard rubber balls that bounce very high. If you take a super ball and throw it against the wall, what happens? It bounces back. What happens the harder you throw it against the wall? It bounces back faster. What happens to a raw egg when you throw it against a wall? It splatters. The harder you throw it against the wall, the worse it splatters. People who set goals for themselves and continue to work hard to reach them, bounce back. The harder the obstacle, the harder they bounce back *(Character Education).*

Be the best you can be. You cannot let obstacles, or things that are hard for you, discourage you. You must be like a super ball and bounce back, continuing to give your best. Your goals (what you want to accomplish) should be extremely important to you. Be the best me you can be.

Dear God,

Help us not to get discouraged, but to work harder to be the best we can be. You have made us in a great way and You have great plans for each of us.

Day 10

"I will take care of myself by getting enough rest."

Now that you are back in school, I'm sure your schedule has changed quite a bit. A good schedule is extremely important in helping you get enough rest, and in helping you succeed in school. You might wonder why your mom and dad make you have the same bedtime every single night. It's no fun having to go to bed on a schedule, especially if you're not tired. However, they have a reason for sending you to bed when they do.

Think of all the things you do in one day. Most kids wake up and go to school. They do all their school work and then they have homework. Once school work is over, they might go outside and play, and of course, there are chores and other responsibilities they have to handle.

That equals a lot of things for one person. Once all this is done, the average body is tired and ready for some relaxation. Your body needs to be able to calm down from a long day and get ready for the next one tomorrow.

Sleep will not only help you to stay healthy, but it also will keep you smart. Sleep affects nearly every part of your body, even your brain. So when your parents insist that you need to get enough sleep, listen to them. It's very important to get the rest you need—it affects everything you do.

Dear God,

We know that You have given us our bodies and that we have a responsibility to do what we can to keep them healthy. Help us to use wisdom and to do what we need to in order to keep ourselves healthy.

Day 11
Patriots Day

"Thank God for our great country and for all those who work so hard to protect it and make it great."

Today we remember all of our First-Responders. Those are the people like the firefighters, policemen, medics and all those who respond in emergency situations.

We also remember those who are in the military, helping to keep our country safe. This is a day to remember that many times people do very dangerous work to make sure that others are kept safe in our country.

We have a very special symbol, the United States flag, to remind us of this great country we live in and all those who work to protect it.

Listen to this poem about our very special flag: *Please sit down, everyone, I'm going to tell a story, About our country's famous flag, It's nickname is Old Glory, Stars and stripes are on our flag, They're red and white and blue, It tells the world that we are free, And proud to be here too (Flag Day Poetry).*

So take some time today to thank God for our great country and for all those who work so hard during difficult times to make it great.

Dear God,

Thank You for this great country that we live in. Thank you for all those men and women who work so hard to keep us safe doing very dangerous jobs

Day 12

"Most of the things worth doing in the world had been declared impossible before they were done."
—Louis D. Brandeis

What does the above Thought for the Day mean? It means that before difficult things were done, most people felt that they could never be done because they were so hard to do. They didn't have faith that anyone could actually do them.

Think about things we've done like flying a plane, going to the moon, curing many diseases, just to mention a few. Men and women have done miraculous things that most people felt could never be done.

So what's the point of this quote? If someone hadn't pursued and continued to make an attempt to do these things, and had given up, most people would still feel they couldn't be done.

You know, when Jesus walked upon this earth, He did miracle after miracle. He did things no one thought could be done—but He was Jesus, wasn't He? But you know what? He has empowered us to do the impossible as well, as long as we keep our eyes on Him. When we focus on Christ, He gives us the power to conquer the impossible. When we lose our focus, He gives us the grace to try again.

We can do all things through Christ who gives us strength. Believe in yourself by keeping your eyes on the Lord. If you do, you will do great things in this life—even things that may seem impossible to others.

Dear God

Thank You for loving us and giving us the potential to do great things in this life. Help us to keep our focus on You and Your purpose for us. Help us to do the impossible, Lord, and to give You all the glory.

Day 13

"An angry man opens his mouth and shuts his eyes."
—Cato, the Elder

Now exactly what does our Thought for Today mean? Well, have you ever been really angry before? I'd say most of us would say yes to that question. Well, what happens when you get really angry? When someone is angry, they do not think about what they are saying before they say it and they do not see how much they are hurting others with their words.

So an angry man opens his mouth and says hurtful things and shuts his eyes and doesn't see the people he is hurting with his words. That is never a good thing.

When we get angry, we need to calm down and pray that God will help us control what we say so that we don't say something unkind to others. This is important because when our anger takes over, we say things that we don't mean to say because we are not using our minds to help us choose our words wisely.

So the next time you get angry about something, stop and ask the Lord to help you choose your words carefully. In fact, don't say anything until you have had time to calm down and redirect your thoughts in the right direction—a direction that is pleasing to the Lord.

Dear God,

Help us, Lord, to monitor our words carefully each and everyday, and especially when we get angry. Help us to not sin against You by saying hurtful things to others. Help us to always ask for Your help and to do the right thing in every situation.

Day 14

"When I am disappointed, I will find ways to keep that disappointment from making me feel sad."

When things don't turn out the way you hoped they would, it may seem like the end of the world to you. However, there are some things you can do to keep disappointment from getting you down. Someone once listed the following seven things to help us when we are sad:

1. "Stop and calm down. Tomorrow things may not seem so bad.
2. Find a way to express what you are feeling without hurting anyone.
3. Talk about it with your parents.
4. Ask yourself if this is really worth you getting so upset about.
5. If your disappointment is due to something you didn't succeed in, ask yourself what you can learn from your mistakes to help you do it correctly the next time.
6. Don't be too hard on yourself. Everyone makes mistakes. You are not a failure.
7. Pray and ask God to help you see the good, even in those things that are disappointing."

You know, nothing is going to go the way we want it to all the time. Life isn't like that. As someone once said, "We are imperfect people living in an imperfect world." We can, however, take our disappointments and turn them around for good.

We can have a positive attitude no matter what we are dealing with because we have an awesome God who is working all things for our good.

Dear God,

Help us take our disappointments and turn them around for good. We know You are on our side.

Day 15

"Be like a postage stamp. Stick to something until you get there."
—Josh Billings

Mr. Billings was talking about the trait of perseverance. What is perseverance? It is staying with a job and not giving up on the work ahead of you. It is trying again and again and again. It is being patient and willing to work hard.

Many of you can think back to people in history that you have studied and you can come up with many examples of those who kept trying and who worked hard to complete the jobs before them. Listen to this list of ways that you can show perseverance:

1. "When you are near the end of a race and struggling to finish, find a burst of energy to cross the finish line.
2. Try a new sport or skill that is difficult for you and don't quit.
3. Study and work hard to improve your grades.
4. Save up your money and do extra chores to buy something special.
5. Help a younger child learn to ride a bicycle or play a new game.
6. Spend some time practicing something you want to learn.
7. Always finish what you start. Do not give up when things get tough.
8. Try something again, even if you failed the first time. Remember you had to learn to walk before you could run" *(Schools.cms).*

It takes perseverance to fulfill your dreams.

Dear God,

Help us to stay with those things that we have started and to never give up.

Day 16

"If we have positive, happy thoughts, this will improve how we think about ourselves and what we can do."

We do not realize how powerful having the right attitude can be. Our attitude determines how successful we will be as students and how well we get along with our classmates.

If we have a good attitude about something, we typically have good results. If, on the other hand, we have a negative or bad attitude or feel that something will turn out badly, it usually does.

We should start to improve our attitude toward ourselves by doing our best at everything we do. Doing our best creates self-confidence, or believing in ourselves.

Someone once compared a positive attitude to electricity because of how powerful it can be in our success. So today, instead of seeing the bad things, try looking for the good. I bet you will have a much better day if you do.

Dear God,

Help us to have a good attitude today and to see the good in each situation. Help us to do our best always, knowing that this is what You expect of each of us.

Day 17

"If I need help, I need to remember not to be afraid to ask for it. I always have many people around me who want to help me."

All of you can remember a time when you needed help with something. Sometimes we need help with very simple things, but sometimes some things may be bothering us that we need to talk to someone about, and that's a little more involved.

What you need to keep in mind is that you don't need to be afraid to ask for help when you need help. Remember, it's okay to ask for help. Don't be embarrassed and don't worry about what other people think.

Stop and think about what might happen if you ***don't*** get help. Now think about how much better it would be if you ***do***.

Decide what the problem is and what help you need. Think about ***who*** you can ask for help. Choose someone you trust and who will know how to help you. Think about what you'll say when you ask for help and then do it.

Remember, getting help when you need it is part of being responsible—to yourself. It's what God would want you to do.

Dear God,

Help us to be willing to ask for help when we need it and to always rely upon You to help us as we seek your wisdom and counsel.

Day 18

"In order to have friends, I must be kind to others."

Each day when you come to school, you put a smile on your face as you see your friends come in, and when you leave in the afternoon, you take the time to say goodbye to those same friends. That's very special because you have a special tie with both old and new friends as the school year goes on.

Having friends is very special. However, the only way we can have friends is to act in a kind way toward others. You need to remember to treat others the way you would want to be treated and that will help you make more and more friends.

Listen to this short poem about friends: *We've joined together as classmates, As the new school year begins. A year full of learning, While we become friends. We'll share and be kind, As we work and we play, And our friendship will grow, With each passing day.*

Remember, in order to have friends, you must be a friend.

Dear God,

Help us to remember to be kind to others and to cherish those friendships we have already made this year. Remind us that in order to have friends, we must treat others kindly.

Day 19

"When things do not work out the way I want them to,
I need to stop and ask God what I can do to make them better."

All of us have good and bad days, don't we? Sometimes everything goes just the way we want it to, but sometimes things do not go the way we think they should.

Maybe we don't get to do what we want, or maybe someone else is chosen to do something that we wanted to do. Sometimes we just feel disappointed because what we wanted to happen didn't happen.

We have all experienced these feelings. However, rather than get upset, we need to stop and ask God for help in dealing with these situations. We need to ask Him what we can do to make things better. We can be a good example during these times by the way we respond.

We should never show an ungodly attitude. Instead, we should depend upon God to help us respond the way we should in these circumstances.

Dear God,

Help us to depend upon You and Your wisdom to make difficult situations for us better. Help us to be good examples for You when things don't go the way we want them to.

Day 20

"It is okay to laugh at funny things,
but it is not okay to laugh at others."

The principal got up in the assembly and she walked up to the microphone and began to talk to the students. Everyone burst out in laughter. She had a fake mustache pasted above her mouth. She wanted to give the students something to laugh about on this particular day, and she certainly accomplished what she wanted to do. Every student in the assembly laughed at their principal that day and that was okay.

However, it is ***never*** okay to laugh at other people who are not trying to be funny. It is ***never*** okay to "make fun of" others, either what they are doing or how they look. God does not want us to laugh at other people and be unkind. This is not His will for us.

So if you get tempted to laugh at other people, stop, think, pray, and ask God to keep you from making a big mistake. Do the right thing.

Dear God,

Help us to remember to be kind to other people and to not be tempted to laugh at others. Help us stay focused on You and what You would have us do in each situation.

Day 21

"We should always strive to be good witnesses for the Lord."

Do you know what a witness is? A witness is someone who has knowledge of something. Someone who knows about something and can tell others about it.

We are witnesses for the Lord when we tell others about Him. But you know, we don't always have to talk about the Lord to be good witnesses. We can be good witnesses for Him by the way we act, and what we do.

Whenever you stop to pray for someone else, others see that. They see that we aren't ashamed to pray to God. Whenever you stop to help someone else, others see that as well. You are speaking loudly through your actions.

Start this day off by being good witnesses for the Lord. As the day progresses, continue to be good witnesses for Him by being kind to others, helpful, respectful, and obedient. Do what the Lord would have you do. You are witnessing to others just by the way you act. Be a good witness.

Dear God,

Help us to be good witnesses for You each and everyday. Help us to remember that sometimes our actions speak much louder than words. Help us to show others that we know and love You by the way we act.

Day 22

"I am doing what God wants me to do when I volunteer to help others."

Have you ever volunteered to help someone do something? Don't you feel good after you do that? Helping others shows them that we care about them and it says a lot about the kind of person we are. When we volunteer our time to do something for someone else, God is pleased because we are taking the spotlight off of us and putting it on someone else.

So try it today. If you see that your teacher needs help doing something, or one of your friends needs your help, volunteer to help them out. Recently, a student asked her principal if she would go get her backpack for her because she had accidentally left it in the hallway when all the students were assembling in the auditorium at the start of the day. The principal went to get the backpack for her, but just as she got back to the door to go get it, another student had gotten it for her friend and was bringing it in to her. This student was being thoughtful and kind and she wanted to help her classmate. God was pleased with her.

So let's all pitch in and help one another when we can. It will make your day better. That's a promise!

Dear God,

Help us to do what we need to do today to please You. If we see someone who needs help, guide us to volunteer to help them out. May we think of others first, and ourselves second.

OCTOBER

Day 1

"What I say and how I say it shows others the kind of person that I am."

Our words are very powerful, aren't they? Have you ever said something you wished you hadn't said? We all have. Our words hurt other people if they are not kind words.

And just like our words can hurt others, our words can build others up too. Most of the time, if you speak kind words to others, it is obvious that you are a kind person.

Likewise, if you speak ugly words to others, this says that, perhaps, you are not as kind a person as you need to be. That's not good, is it?

Listen to this short poem about our words: *What I say and how I say it, Can make or break someone's day. It can put a smile on their face, Or it can make their joy completely fade away. God is pleased with kind words we speak, He looks at us with a smile of love, He never wants our words to be mean, But rather words that we are proud of.*

So think today about the fact that what you say, and how you say it, truly tells others a lot about the kind of person you are. You want to be the person that God wants you to be.

Here is a challenge for each and every one of you. Make God happy today by speaking words that He will be proud of.

Dear God,

Help us to remember to be careful of what we say and how we say it so that we don't hurt others. Help us remember that what we say and how we say it, says a lot about the person we are.

Day 2

"What we are is God's gift to us.
What we become is our gift to God."
—Eleanor Powell

God has given us all so many wonderful gifts. Each of us has been wonderfully blessed.

He has given us our abilities and talents, our families, our friends, our school; and those things working together make us who we are. These are gifts that God blesses us with.

However, if we want to give back to God, we have a responsibility to use those things to become the person He wants us to be. He gave them to us for a reason and He expects us to use them to glorify Him.

When we take the gifts He has given us and use them to become the person He wants us to be, we are presenting Him a gift in return. That's His purpose for us—for us to use what He has blessed us with to become the person He designed us to be.

So remember to first think about all the wonderful gifts God has given you, and then think about the ways you can use those to present a gift to God.

Dear God,

You have blessed each of us so richly and have given each of us so many wonderful gifts and abilities. Lord, help us to use those things You have given us to present to You a gift of honor as we become the people You want us to be.

Day 3

"When I smile at people, they usually smile back."

Sometime during this school year you will be having your yearly picture day. What is the one thing that photographers normally tell you to do before you have your picture taken?

That's right. They normally tell you to smile at the camera, right? Now obviously, a camera can't smile back at you, but you smile at the camera anyway because your picture looks better if you are smiling in it.

Now think about our Thought for the Day—"When I smile at people, they usually smile back." I bet there are very few people that you have smiled at who have not smiled back at you. So, just as you are told to smile at the camera when you have your picture taken, try smiling at your classmates, your teachers, the office staff, or anyone you come in contact with. I bet you will get a smile right back. This is your assignment today—see what happens when you smile at someone. You already know the answer.

So when you have your picture made this year, smile for the camera, yes, but don't stop there. Smile at the photographer, your teacher, your classmates—smile at everyone you see. I bet you will be pleasantly surprised at what your smile will do for someone else.

Dear God,

Help us today to remember to be kind and gracious and to smile at others because we never know how a smile might brighten someone else's day.

Day 4

"I will try to learn something new each day."

It is hard to believe, but just since the beginning of this school year, you have already learned so very much. Can you imagine if you took this

Thought for the Day and truly tried to learn something new each day? What would that mean for you?

You would know a lot of different things, wouldn't you? You should never stop learning. No matter how smart you are, or how old you are, you can always learn new things. Never stop trying to learn new things.

You know, your teachers are really smart, aren't they? However, probably if you asked them, they would tell you that they are still learning new things all the time.

We never want to stop learning. Always remember, whatever you learn can never be taken away from you no matter what. Keep it going! Keep learning. Learn something new everyday!

Dear God,

Thank You for all the opportunities You give us to use the gifts You have bestowed upon us. Lord, You have gifted each of us with a mind to learn. Help us learn of You and Your greatness and to learn about the things You have placed upon this earth for us to enjoy.

Help us to enjoy learning and to strive to learn more each day. Help us learn more about You and more about the things our teachers have for us in the classroom.

Day 5

"I appreciate my family, my teachers, and my school."

We all know how blessed we are by God to have all that we have. However, it would be a wonderful idea if you just went up to your mom and dad this afternoon after you get home, and thanked them for all they do for you. You might even want to go up to your teacher today and tell them that you appreciate all they do each day to help you learn the things you need to learn.

It is also wonderful to have a school to come to where we can learn about God while we are learning about all the other things we need to know. Not everyone has this same learning environment. We are very blessed.

So today, make this a day when you let those who are such an important part of your life know how much you love and appreciate them. We are totally blessed by God. Let's show our appreciation.

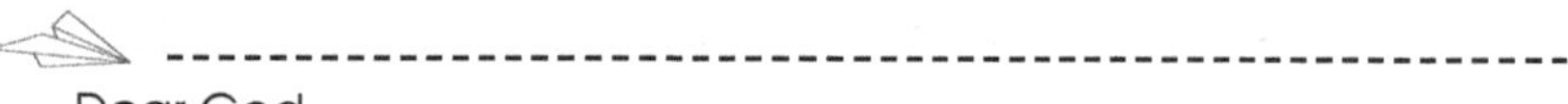

Dear God,

You have blessed us with so much. We pray that we will never take your goodness for granted and that we will always stop to thank You, as well, for all that You do for us.

Help us to be mindful of all those who do so much for us. Help us to show them that we appreciate their kindness toward us.

Day 6

"I will remember that my words, the choices I make, and my actions will make a difference, not only in my life, but in the lives of others."

We talk often about respect, responsibility, and caring for others. These three character traits are extremely important and God wants us to show these traits everyday. A lady named Carol McCloud used the following illustration to help us all remember to exhibit these traits daily:

"Think about a large sand bucket. Think about being on the beach and filling it with sand. You know what? Everyone in your class carries an invisible bucket. It is either empty or full. You can either be a bucket-filler or a bucket-dipper. Being respectful, responsible, and caring to others will fill their buckets. Not showing these characteristics takes away from their buckets. Saying unkind words to others or treating them badly takes away from their bucket."

Fill others' buckets with kind words, compliments, or special thoughts. Tell someone what you like about them today. Fill their bucket. Be a bucket-filler and show good character. You know, when you fill others' buckets, you feel much better about yourself. It makes ***you*** happy as well.

So today, think about what you can do to fill someone's bucket. Think happy thoughts—be responsible, respectful, and caring. Your bucket will fill up each time you fill someone else's. It's the right thing to do.

Dear God,

Help all of us to concentrate on doing the right thing. Help us to look for the good in others and to strive to build them up, not tear them down.

Day 7

"I am blessed to have my family and to know that God loves me and my family."

Aren't we blessed to have our families? Did you know that God created families so that we could love each other, and take care of each other?

Everyone in a family is important. God loves all the members of your family and it is good for ***us*** to love our family members, too. In fact, how could we not love our family members? They are such an important part of our lives.

You, as a child, are a very important part of your family. The Bible says that "children are a gift from God". Did you ever think of yourself as a gift? That's an interesting thought—you are each a ***gift*** from God.

Everyone in a family has different jobs to do. Did you know that as a child you have a job to do? The Bible says that "children are to obey their parents". What does the word, obey, mean? Obey means to do what you are asked by your parents. That's your job for now.

Parents have a job, too. Parents are to love and care for their children—you. This is another reason that God made families.

Aren't we glad we have a family? Aren't we glad that God loves our family? What a wonderful blessing He has given each of us when He gave us the blessing of family.

Dear God,

Thank you for the blessing of family. What a gift You have given each of us. Help us to show those in our families how much we love them and help us to do those things You want us to do to be a blessing to those in our families.

Day 8

"I need to get to know others who are different from me."

How are we alike? How are we different? Have you ever wondered what life is like in someone else's shoes? No one really knows what someone else's life is like unless they "walk a mile in their shoes", as the saying goes.

This means that everyone's life experiences are unique and that no one can know exactly what someone else's life is like unless they tell them. Considering this, it also means that we should try to understand someone else before judging them or criticizing them.

We are all uniquely made and, yes, many people are very different from us, ***but*** we should be willing to get to know those who are not like us and look at their qualities in a positive way. Remember that God created all of us individually, and we are all special.

Don't be afraid to get to know someone just because they are different from you. It's those differences that make us all unique and remarkable people of God.

Dear God,

Thank You for the differences that You have instilled in each of us. We know that You have a plan for each of those differences, and that they will help to complete Your purpose in each person's life. Help us to be willing to get to know those who are different from us and to realize that they are very special because You have made them in your unique way.

Day 9

"I believe that I am someone who can do important things."

Have you ever thought about what you might want to do when you grow up? We all have an idea of what we might like to do in the future. If you haven't thought about it, you will.

You know, God has great plans for each one of you. In Jeremiah 29:11, it says, "I know the plans I have for you," declares the Lord, "Plans to prosper you and not to harm you, plans to give you hope and a future."

So the Thought for the Day emphasizes that you need to believe that you can do important things. You need to believe in yourself because God believes in you and He already has plans for you.

You just need to have the confidence that if God has a plan for you, you are someone important in His eyes. You all can do great things with His help. Never leave Him out of your plans.

Those who know you certainly look forward to seeing what God is going to do in each of you in the future.

Dear God,

Help us to believe in ourselves and to know that, with Your help, we can do very important things in the future. Help us to never take our focus off of You.

Day 10

"I will celebrate God's goodness."

God's goodness is all around us. Look at what the Lord has done for you already:

1. He has put people in your life who love you.
2. Often those people who love you, make great sacrifices to ensure that you have what you need to come to school everyday.
3. He has given you teachers who care about you and who want what's best for you.
4. And God's goodness is seen in the fact that He has provided a way for us to be with Him in heaven one day.
5. Never forget to celebrate God's goodness. It is all around us everyday. He is our awesome God.

Dear God,

We praise You and thank You for Your goodness to us. Help us to be mindful of all that You give us daily.

Day 11

"I should not gossip; If I cannot say anything helpful, I will not say anything at all."

Do you know what it means to gossip? It means that we talk about others to other people. And, it is in a negative or bad way. All of us have done this, haven't we? We are all guilty.

In many school handbooks, it specifically lists gossiping as something we should never do because it creates hard feelings between you and your classmates. It is a really hurtful thing to do because many times what we say isn't really truthful and we are just saying it to hurt someone else. We don't want to get in the habit of doing this because it is wrong and it is not what God wants us to be doing.

So, start today and tell yourself that you will not say anything if you can't say something good about others. Never gossip about others. Instead, say something nice or don't say anything at all.

Dear God,

Help us to do the right thing today. Keep us from gossiping about others. Instead, help us to look for nice things we can say about other people.

Day 12

"Jesus should be our special best friend."

Jesus should be our best friend because He knows us better than anyone else. He is God, and He knows all about us. He even knows our thoughts. When you are thinking something in your classroom, He knows what you are thinking.

We are very important to Jesus! We may not be important to some people, but Jesus really cares for us. He even knows how many hairs we have on our head. He has them all numbered.

A best friend is one who loves us just the way we are, and yet helps us to be all we can be. Jesus is our special best friend because no one has ever loved us so much that they gave their life for us. In addition, He loves us today, just as much as He did then. No matter what we do that disappoints Him, He will forgive us.

Someone once said that "The Lord Jesus loves us just the way we are, but He loves us too much to leave us the way we are." When He lives in us, He makes us more like Himself day-by-day.

He knows what we don't do well, but He loves us and He will never take His love away from us. Isn't that special? What a wonderful best friend we all have.

Dear God,

Thank you for being our "special best friend". Thank You for being near everyday so we can talk with You and ask You for help. Help us to always be aware of Your presence and to rely upon Your wisdom to help us do the right thing.

Day 13

"God never changes."

We are all aware of the fact that there are many things in our lives that change. People grow older, friends come and go, and what we do and when we do it always changes.

But no matter what else may change, God is good and He never changes. God loves us forever no matter what our circumstances and that will never change.

As human beings, that sometimes is hard for us to understand because we see people changing and things changing all the time. Sometimes change can even be scary or cause us to worry.

But there is one thing that we can always count on: God does ***not*** change!!! Isn't that wonderful? God does not change—***Ever***!!!!

The Bible teaches us that Jesus Christ is the same yesterday, today, and forever. God loves us and nothing will ever separate us from that love.

God loves us when we're happy and sad. He loves us whether we are scared or mad. God loves us all the time. Since God never changes, that means that God will love us forever and ever.

Isn't that a good thing to know? Even if lots of things change around us, even if we change, God always loves us and God does ***not*** change.

Dear God,

Thank You for being our God and for loving us so completely. Thank You for being an unchanging God who is the same forever.

Day 14

"Help is everywhere. I only need to ask."

Think about something that you need help to do. Now, think about the last time you had to ask for help.

All of us have things that are hard for us to do. However, when something is hard, we first need to ***try*** to do it. We don't just ***assume*** we can't do it. We need to try first. You won't know if you can do it until you try.

If you can't do it after you've tried, the responsible thing to do is to ask for help. Say to yourself, "I need help." Decide who to ask for help. Think about whether or not a friend can help you or if you need to ask a teacher.

Use kind words to ask. People are more willing to help us if we ask in a kind way.

The chances are, that you may only ask one person to help you, but, in reality, you may end up with many people working to help you. We are a school family and we work daily to help one another.

So if you find you need help, ask for help. Help is all around you—you only have to ask.

Dear God,

Help us not to be afraid to ask for help when we need it and to allow others to help us. Help us to help others as well when we can.

Day 15

"When I find something that belongs to someone else, I will do my best to return it to the person it belongs to. This is what I would want others to do for me."

Have you ever lost something that is important to you? I bet you looked everywhere to try to find it. Normally, the first thing you think is: "I want it back!"

When you found it, if you did, did it happen to be because someone else found it and returned it to you? If so, how did that make you feel? I bet if someone else found the item and brought it to you, you really appreciated the fact that they cared enough to bring it back to you.

Now, let's think about that. What if ***you*** find something that belongs to someone else. What should you do? Of course, you should do your best to get it to the person that it belongs to. You know how you would feel if you were in the same situation so you need to do the same thing for others. It's the right thing to do.

Dear God,

Help us to stop and think about doing the right thing. Help us to remember that we need to do unto others as we would have them do unto us.

Day 16

"We need to talk to God throughout the day in prayer. He is our truest friend and we need to talk with our friend often."

If you were asked the question, "Do you like to talk to others?" there is no doubt that most of you would immediately answer, "Yes!" What would our lives be like if we couldn't talk with others?

Talking with people is important to us. Most of us, call or text others when we need to, and make sure that others can get in touch with us, too.

So if talking to people is easy, and we do it all the time, how much more important it is to talk to God during our day. More than that, it is even easier to talk to God than it is to call or text someone else.

Why is it so important to talk with God? Someone once offered the following simple list to express why it is so important to talk to God in prayer:

1. "We get to know God better through prayer.
2. God wants to listen to us and answer our prayers.

3. God loves us through prayer.
4. We show God our love through prayer."

Remember that it's as simple as talking to someone you love—because this someone loves you more than you'll ever know. Talk to God often!

Dear God

Help us to talk with You more and to depend on Your guidance to help us through each day.

Day 17

"I will use my words to build others up today."

Think of a time when someone said something that made you feel really good. Now, think of a time when someone said something to you that did not make you feel so good.

Obviously, you can see from these questions that our words make a difference in people's lives. They affect those around us. The words we say have power to make people feel a certain way. Because of that, we must always use our words to build people up.

There are helpful words and there are hurtful words. Our words should always be helpful. Christ wants us to love one another. To do this, we must always stop and think before we speak. That's not always easy to do, is it? However, when we stop, that gives us time to ask the Lord to help us not say anything unkind to others. Instead, use words that build others up and put a smile on their face. That way, you can almost guarantee that you will have a smile on your face as well.

Dear God,

Help us to use our words to build others up and to encourage those that we come in contact with.

Day 18

"Sports and games are for fun. When I lose in a game,
I am still happy for being able to participate and have fun."

Isn't it fun to play games? There are all kinds of games we often play. There are card games, board games, games we play in our gym classes, and many of you play different sports. Playing different games is so much fun.

But you know, someone has to lose, don't they? Everyone can't win every game. We need to accept the fact that we can't win every time. We need to focus on the fact that we have fun ***just playing*** the game. That's a time to connect with our friends and just have a good time.

So when you lose in one of these games, keep a smile on your face and congratulate those who win. Everyone wins when you do that.

Dear God,

Thank you for giving us the ability to participate in different activities. Lord, remind us that whether we win or lose, having the right attitude is what really matters.

Help us to be good sports always and to be good examples for You. Thank you, God, for being such a good sport for us.

Day 19

"Everyone makes mistakes. It is what we do with those mistakes that make the difference."

Our Thought for the Day is an important reminder for all of us because we all make mistakes all the time. No one does everything right all the time. It is what we do when we make a mistake that makes the difference.

We've all heard the story, *The Little Engine That Could.* Well, what did the little engine tell himself? He said, "I think I can, I think I can, I think I can."

Do you ever get discouraged or frustrated? When you give up easily, how do you feel? When something is hard, but you keep trying, how do you feel? What is one of the most difficult things you have ever done?

These are good questions for you to ask yourself because it makes you think about what you should and should not do when you make mistakes. You don't give up—you keep trying and learn from what you did wrong.

You know, a mistake can be a beautiful thing ***if*** you learn from it.

Listen to this short poem: *Mistakes can be good. They can help you grow. They can show you what you need to know. So whenever you make a mistake, Just say: "Now I'll try another way" (Judy Lalli).*

Dear God,

Help us to remember that we are human and we are going to make mistakes. Lord, help us to keep trying and to never give up when we have something that is difficult for us. Help us to learn from our mistakes and to make something good from them.

Day 20

"I will tell others what I like about them."

Have you ever done what our Thought for the Day says? Have you ever told others what you like about them? You know, we have friends with us all day long and each of you know what you like about your friends. However, have you ever just told them what you like about them?

I bet that if you tried that, it would make their day. What if you went up to your friend and said, "I like that you are so helpful to other people." I bet that would put a big smile on their face. Or if you said, "I like that you are always willing to listen to what I have to say." Again, you don't know how good that would make them feel.

If someone said those things to you, I bet you would feel wonderful, wouldn't you? Why not focus on the good things that you like about those around you and try telling them. I bet that would encourage them to keep doing those good things and make them feel really good inside.

Your friends will appreciate the fact that you took the time to look at the positive things about them. Why not try this today? You never know, maybe someone will turn this around on you and you will hear what they like about you as well. This can be a great start to your day!

Dear God,

Help us to focus on positive things, Lord. Not only with our friends and classmates, but in all things—help us look for the good and to encourage those around us with our positive attitude.

Day 21

"You can count on me. When I promise to do something, I do it (as long as I do not hurt myself or others)."

Think of some promises that others have made to you. Has anyone ever let you down by not keeping their promise? How did that make you feel? I bet you were disappointed, frustrated, somewhat angry, and even discouraged.

What about you? Have you ever made a promise and then you didn't do what you said you would do?

When someone makes a promise, we expect that person to keep it. We have a good example to follow because we know from the Bible that there is someone who says, "I promise" and He always keeps the promise. That is the Lord.

Just as the Lord keeps His promises, if we tell someone we are going to do something, we need to follow through with it. If we don't, they will never believe us again when we make a promise.

Promises are special. Promises should be so special to us that we will strive to our utmost to never break them. That is what God wants from each of us. He wants us to see promises just as He sees them—a special declaration that you will follow through with what you say you will do.

Dear God,

Help us to always be people of our word. Help us to always strive to keep our promises. Help us to speak truth and to be an encouragement to others.

Day 22

"Jesus wants us to obey Him."

Jesus wants us to obey Him each and everyday. He doesn't want us to just obey Him when we are in school and your teacher is reminding you to obey or when your parents are saying this daily. It means when you are alone or with others; it means ***all the time***. Obey the Lord and do what He wants you to do ***always***.

As we think of all that the Lord has done for us, we want to love Him with all our heart. This brings joy to the Lord's heart. And the way to bring joy to His heart is by obeying Him. Jesus said, "If you love me, keep my commandments."

The Lord tells us things that we should not do, but sometimes when we are alone or thinking that no one will see, we tend to do things we shouldn't. We forget that Jesus sees and knows all things. We need to obey God always, not just when others are watching.

We please the Lord when we obey the right way, with the right attitude. So as you are enjoying your day today, remember that it will be even better if you obey the Lord and do what He wants you to do ***all the time***.

Dear God,

Help us to be obedient to Your word. Help us to strive to be the best we can be always and to be the example for others that You want us to be.

Day 23

"The best way to cheer yourself up is to try to cheer somebody else up."
—Mark Twain

The meaning of our Thought for the Day is very simple: When you make others feel better, then you will feel better too. Most of the time, this is not a very hard thing to do.

Helping others feel better is one of the most wonderful blessings you can give others. When you help others feel better, you too, are receiving a gift from helping them.

It is a great way to feel better yourself. Sometimes ***we*** need what we are giving to others. If they need a smile, give them a smile and then both of you will feel better inside. Both of you will smile because what you give, you will receive many times over.

What is another way you could cheer someone else up? Sometimes just being a friend to them can cheer others up. Happiness is an emotion that needs to be shared.

Give them a smile and then just listen to them and be their friend. When you do this, something happens inside of you. ***You*** start to feel good because you have helped someone else feel better.

All at once, you find yourself feeling better and you are cheered up too. Try it!

Dear God,

Help us to look for ways to cheer others up and to help them feel better. Help us to be good examples and to always strive to do the right thing.

Day 24

"I will speak only kind words, or no words at all."

Do you ever recall a time in the Bible when Jesus said something ugly to someone? The answer is, "No." He only spoke kind words and showed people He loved them. That is how He wants us to be.

He would much prefer that we keep our mouths closed rather than say something unkind. We hurt others when we do that.

Each day we have an opportunity to be a good example for our friends in this regard. If they are talking about someone in a negative way, why not say something kind about them? This may change the whole direction of the conversation.

Remember this today: If you are tempted to say something unkind to someone, or about someone, close your mouth and pray that God will help you to be nice instead. He will be smiling down upon you and He will help you to say only those things that will make others smile as well.

Dear God,

When we are tempted to say things to others that are not kind, help us remember that these things hurt others.

Help us to hold our tongues. Help us to do what is right today and always.

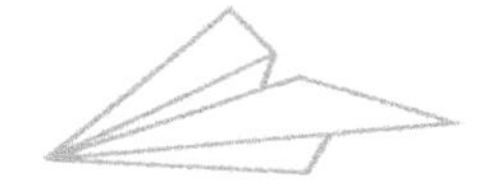

NOVEMBER

Day 1

"I will say 'no' to things that are wrong,
even if others don't agree with me."

You know, it takes a lot of courage to be the only one in a group of friends who refuses to do what others are doing because it is wrong. You may have those in the group who get mad at you because you don't want to go along with what they want to do. You have to be strong.

However, this is what God expects of each of us. If you see your classmates doing something in the classroom that you know your teacher disapproves of, do you tend to go along with them or do you say, "I'm not doing that because it is not the right thing to do."?

Most of you would make the right decision and stand up for what is right. The earlier you start doing that the better it will be for you, because in life, you will always be faced with making the right decision, even if it is not the popular one with your friends.

So remember, when you are faced with doing something you are not sure is right, ask yourself how God would feel about it and then have the courage to stand up and say, "No, I'm not doing that because it's wrong." You may give others the courage to say "no" as well.

You can be a leader for good. God's leader.

Dear God,

Help us to do what is right today and to stand up and say "no" to those things you would not approve of.

Day 2

"I am grateful for what I have so I will share with others."

God has given all of us so many wonderful blessings. We all have so much to be grateful for.

We often hear stories about so many people who have so much and because they have been blessed so mightily, they want to share their blessings with others. That's great, isn't it? By sharing our blessings, we are, in a sense, giving back to the Lord because we are helping others.

One of the greatest things we can do is share our good things with other people. After all, we didn't do anything to earn those things, did we? God gave them to us freely.

When we take those things and share them with others, we are honoring God. So whether it is sharing a pencil, a crayon, a cookie, or whatever, remember to share what you have with others.

Listen to this poem about sharing: *Sharing is taking what's useful to one, And making it useful by two. It can be hard, To give up what you have, But it shows that you care, When you do (Author Anonymous).*

Dear God,

Help us take our focus off ourselves today and to put it on others. Help us to look for opportunities to share our blessings with those around us. May the wonderful feeling that we get from doing that, inspire us to do that more.

Day 3

"I will be careful what I promise."

Promises are very special, aren't they? A promise is a statement telling someone that you will definitely do something or that something will definitely happen in the future.

That's why you need to be careful what you promise because promises are like guarantees that you will do something or that something will happen. If those things don't happen, and you don't do what you say, or something doesn't happen like you promised, that promise has been broken. If you break your promise, it will be hard for others to believe you again when you make another promise.

Listen to this little poem about promises. It says a lot about the importance of keeping our promises:

If I promise to do it, I'll do it. If I promise to go, I'll be there. If I promise to finish, I'll finish. Keeping my word shows I care (Judy Lalli).

You need to always be a person who keeps their promises because when you do, you are showing others that you care enough about them to do what you have said you would do.

Dear God,

Help us to be people of our word. Help us to keep our promises and to not promise things when we can't do them.

Day 4

"I will not make fun of others because God has created us all equally. We are all special in His sight."

In most Christian school handbooks, there is usually a reminder to all students that they should be respectful of others and demonstrate a Christ-like attitude at all times. This reminder is there for a very important reason. Simply put, it is something everyone should strive to do daily, wherever they are.

If you make fun of other people, you are certainly not demonstrating a Christ-like attitude because the Lord would never make fun of others or say ugly things about others. This is not what He wants anyone to do.

If you do this, He is certainly not happy with this behavior. So if you get tempted to say something about someone else, or make fun of someone else, stop and think; they were created by the Lord and He thinks they are very special, so we should too.

Dear God,

Help us to do what is right today. Help us to remember that You have created all of us equally and that we are all Your children.

Day 5

"Love the Lord your God with all your heart and with all your mind...and love your neighbor as yourself."
—Matthew 22: 36-39

Rules are very important, aren't they? Whether you are at school or at play, there are rules that you are expected to follow. In almost every school classroom, there is a poster on the wall with a list of rules that the teacher expects the students to follow. The following is a list from one of the classroom posters:

- Don't talk when the teacher is talking.
- Don't chew gum.
- Stay in your seat.
- Do your own work.
- Keep your hands to yourself.
- Follow directions.
- Don't talk without permission.
- Listen when someone is speaking.

- Keep your desk neat and clean.
- Be kind and respect one another.

That's a great list of classroom rules, don't you think? Which one of these rules do you think is the most important? Which rule do you think your teacher would think is the most important? Your teacher would probably say that the most important rule is, "Be kind and respect one another."

When Jesus walked on this earth, the people had to follow rules too. Jesus, while on earth, said that the greatest of the Ten Commandments was to "Love the Lord your God with all your heart and with all your soul and with all your mind, … And the second is like it: Love your neighbor as yourself." Jesus was saying that if we can keep these two commandments, we will not have any trouble keeping any of the others.

Dear God,

Help us to love You with all our heart, and to love our neighbor as ourselves.

Day 6

"Jesus loves me."

Jesus loves children! He likes you the way you are because you don't think of yourselves as being the greatest, or feel like you know everything, like some adults do. Most of you believe things about God without trying to figure out everything first.

If, at times, you feel that you aren't as important as other older people, and that no one notices you, remember that you are very important to the greatest king of all: King Jesus! He cares so much about you that He even warned grown-ups: "See that you do not look down on one of these little ones" *(Matthew 18:10).*

In fact, God cares about you so much that He thinks about you all the time. David, the shepherd, wrote in one of his psalms, "How precious to me are your thoughts O God! How vast is the sum of them! Were I to count them, they would outnumber the grains of sand" *(Psalm 139:17-18).*

In regard to this Bible verse, someone once said, "to try to understand how much and how often God thinks about you, think about scooping up a handful of sand and trying to count every grain. If you had a grain of sand for every thought God has about you, how many thoughts do you suppose there would be?" Lots & lots & lots!

Knowing how much God thinks about you should make you feel very loved and very special. Why not talk to the Lord during our prayer and tell Him that you love Him too!

Dear God,

Thank you for Your goodness and mercy. Thank You for the love You show us each and everyday. Help us to remember to let You know how much we love You as well.

Day 7

"Speak when you are angry, and you will make the best speech you will ever regret."
—Ambrose Bierce

What does our Thought for the Day mean? It means that if you don't control your words when you get angry, you will say things you will be sorry you said. You will say hurtful things that you wish you could take back.

None of us want to say things in anger that hurt others or are unkind. God wants us to have self-control. How do you respond when you get angry?

Sometimes we get angry at something or someone. Then we blow up just like a volcano and say some mean and hateful things. Afterwards, we may feel badly about it, but you can never take back your words. You can say you're sorry, but the person you yelled at, even if they forgive you, doesn't forget what you've said.

That's why it's really important to learn to control our anger. Anger is something we do feel sometimes. We can't help but be angry in some situations. However, we can help how we act and what we say. Maybe you've heard someone say, "Count to ten before you do or say anything." That's good advice.

Maybe the best thing you can do is just take some time to pray and trust that God will help you get through whatever it is without hurting others.

Dear God,

Help us to use self-control to respond appropriately when things happen that upset us.

Day 8

"I never, never, never, give up!"

Did you know that many of the smartest people in this country's history didn't get it right the first time they tried something? Many of our most famous inventors had to fail many times before they finally succeeded.

Do you know what made the difference in their success? They kept trying and they didn't get discouraged and give up.

That is something for all of us to remember no matter how young or old we are. We need to keep trying until we are successful in what we are attempting. One of the things that made the most successful people in our history stand out was their will to keep on trying and not to give up.

So if you don't get something right the first time, remind yourself that truly successful people keep trying until they succeed. Each time we don't get it right, we learn something else from that attempt until after enough tries, we will master it.

Keep working and trying—you will get it if you don't give up.

Dear God,

Help us not to get discouraged when we try something and it doesn't work. Instead, Lord, help us to keep trying and never give up until we are successful in what we are trying to do. We know that You help us daily and with Your help we will always be successful in the end.

Day 9

"The way to have a good influence on others is to step up and do something positive. Be a leader for good."

Do you know what influence is? Influence is the ability to have an effect on the behavior of someone or something. Now, we can have an influence for either good or bad, can't we?

Note the term, "Good Positive Influence". We want to be an influence for good on others. Many of you have a natural leadership ability. You are leaders in your classrooms.

However, we want to always be sure that we are leading in the right way. God expects us to be ***good*** leaders. If you are an outgoing person, chances are that you are a leader among your classmates.

You can make a true difference. Make sure you are leading in the right way. Others probably listen to what you say and follow what you do. You want to make sure that all you say and do is what God would have you say and do.

Be a positive influence on others. Lead others the way God would have you lead others.

Dear God,

Help us to lead in the way You would have us lead. Help us to be good influences on all those we come in contact with.

Day 10

"A successful person is someone who hasn't gotten everything right, but who has learned from his mistakes so that he can do it better the next time."

Everyone messes up sometimes, don't they? Every single person has messed up, but each time we mess up, we should learn what we could have done differently to make it better.

Everyone has experienced working on something and not being able to make it work out right. In fact, we have all experienced just messing something up terribly.

We have all also experienced looking at the situation, after we have messed up, and having it occur to us that if we had done certain things differently, it would have probably worked out. We learn from our mistakes.

When we try it again, we correct what we had done so poorly before, use what we have learned, and we find that we have successfully completed what we were attempting. We are successful!

Learn from your mistakes—don't let them get you down. Take them and learn from them. Those who do that are the most successful people.

Dear God,

Help us not to get discouraged when we mess up, but rather, help us learn from our mistakes, try again, and make something great out of something that could have been a negative.

Day 11

"It is a humbling thing to ask why we have been given so much and to realize that God has showered His blessings upon us, even when we don't deserve them."
—Anonymous

Do you know what it means to be humble? It means that we don't think so highly of ourselves. We put others first.

When we really look at how much God has blessed us with, we realize that we truly are not deserving of any of it. However, because He loves us, we are blessed. That's a humbling thought. The Thanksgiving Holiday is drawing close. Start to think about this special time when we stop and reflect on all we have been given. When we do that, we are amazed at how much the Lord has blessed us.

That should make us all so grateful everyday for everything we have. We are so blessed. Don't look at others and ask why they have something you don't. That is a very dangerous thing. Instead, praise God daily for all that He has given you.

Dear God,

Thank You so much for all of our wonderful blessings. Thank You for our families, our teachers, our friends, and our school.

Help us to be grateful for all we have and to always give You the glory for it.

Day 12

"Every artist was first an amateur."
—Ralph Waldo Emerson

All of you know what an artist is, but do you know what an amateur is? An amateur is someone who does something without having had training for it, OR has had training for it, but is still in the learning stage.

What that really means is that everyone has to start somewhere. Just because someone may be great at something they are doing now, doesn't mean that they didn't have to start from the beginning when no one knew who they were.

They had to keep working and getting better and better at what they did in order to do the job the way it needed to be done. They had to practice over, and over, and over.

Everyone has had to learn to do something and that's where "never giving up" comes in. You start at the beginning and you learn as you go until you feel that you can do what you are attempting well.

So the next time you see a picture that someone has painted, remember that they had to learn how to do that. Yes, it may look great when you see it, but there was a lot that went into the picture before the person really took on the title of artist. They had to keep on keeping on. They never gave up!

Dear God,

Help us to do what You would have us do and to do it to the best of our ability. Help us to remember that in order to get better at something, we must keep on trying and never give up!!

Day 13

"Gives thanks to the Lord, for He
is good. His love endures forever."
—Psalm 107:1

These are great words from the Bible. King David of Israel, wrote these words down to praise God with them. David also wrote these words, "I will praise God's name in song and glorify Him with Thanksgiving" (Psalm 69:30). Praising God means saying things to God that are true about Him. When we say things like: "God is good!" that is praising God, because God ***is*** good!

We soon will be celebrating the holiday of Thanksgiving. When we do that, we are setting aside a day to thank God for all the good things He has given to us. We can thank Him for our simple blessings, such as our toys or pets, as well as our big and wonderful blessings, such as our salvation through His son, Jesus Christ.

We can also thank Him for ***anything*** good that we have received because the Bible tells us that He has given us ***every*** good and perfect gift. This entire holiday season should help us focus on our many blessings.

So, as the holiday season approaches, stop and take time to thank God for all of His many blessings because He has certainly blessed us abundantly.

Dear God,

Thank You for all the good and perfect gifts You have given us. We praise You for how good and loving You are! Help us to make everyday a day of Thanksgiving.

Day 14

"When I start to feel unsure of myself,
I will ask God to help me through it."

Do you know what it means to feel unsure of yourself? When you are unsure of yourself, you doubt that you can do something. Do you ever feel that way?

Well, Philippians 4:13 says, "I can do all things through Christ who strengthens me." If you are struggling with doubt, and feel that you may not be able to do something, remember that God is faithful and you must be secure in the fact that He will help you and strengthen you.

Don't let the devil put doubt in your head—God is almighty. When you start to doubt yourself, repeat the verse, "I can do all things through Christ who strengthens me." I bet you will immediately feel His strength.

Dear God,

Thank You for being with us every step of the way in every area of our lives. Thank You for caring enough about our concerns that You will take even something very small and help us to overcome our struggles with it.

Be with us today and increase our faith in the fact that You will strengthen us to face any difficulty.

Day 15

"I need to have good manners. If I do, I will have friends."

We need to remember to have good manners. When we use polite words, such as please, thank you, excuse me, and I'm sorry, we show those around us that we care about how our actions affect others.

Using manners shows respect and consideration for those we come in contact with. It makes others feel appreciated. You can show kindness and respect for other people by speaking politely to them—that's what we mean by using manners.

That is one way we can have good manners, but there are other things we can do to show good manners. Some of these things you may never have thought about.

People who have good manners: *(Taken from Character Building Poster)*

- They don't embarrass other people
- They don't just talk about themselves all the time
- They don't gossip
- They don't stare at other people
- They don't point at others, and
- They don't talk over others

Now going back to our Thought for the Day—using manners helps us have friends—this is because when you are respectful of others by having good manners, they like to be around you, and you will be a person that everyone wants to be friends with.

Dear God,

Help us remember to have good manners throughout our day, and to show respect to others.

Day 16

"Our tongue is powerful. Saying something negative about someone hurts them. I will speak only those things which will build others up. If I talk about someone, I will always say something good."

Our words have life. The words we speak have power so we must be careful of what we say. You can never take back the words from your mouth. You may say that you are sorry for saying them, but you can never take them back.

Every word we speak first started with a thought. The things we think about and allow in our mind can either be helpful or harmful.

Likewise, our actions start with a thought. We need to think before we speak so we need to think good thoughts, rather than bad ones. We need to let the power in our tongue be used to build others up, not tear them down.

Dear God,

Help us to remember how much power our words have today. Help us to think about what we say before we say it and to only say positive, uplifting things to those around us.

Day 17

"'Our bodies are the temple of God' (1 Corinthians 6:19). Because of that, I should take care of my body, eat right, and do everything I can to make sure I stay healthy."

Most of us care about ourselves—and that is very good. Because of that, we should be thoughtful about what is good for us and what is not good for us. We should think about how we take care of our bodies and our minds.

We should eat correctly, get lots of exercise, and challenge ourselves to learn more in school. We should look for ways to stay healthy because we care about our body, the temple of God.

However, there is another reason that we should care about keeping ourselves healthy—other than the fact that our body is God's temple, we should also care about ourselves because our health and happiness affects other people.

Our families love us and want us to be healthy and happy. If we don't take care of ourselves, our families hurt. They worry about us.

Why do they worry about us? Because they love us, and God loves us even more than that. So take care of yourself and make everyone happy.

Dear God,

Make us aware of how important it is to take care of ourselves. We know that You have made us special and have given us these wonderful bodies. Help us to do what we can to take care of ourselves the way we need to.

Day 18

Thanksgiving

"I will be thankful and give God praise for all He has given to me, while remembering those less fortunate."

You know, Thanksgiving is a beautiful holiday. Everywhere you look you see Thanksgiving decorations and they are beautiful.

However, sometimes, as we get caught up in the spirit of the holiday, we forget that a lot of people in this world have very little. They are not as blessed as we are.

Sometimes it is easy to take God's goodness for granted and we forget about those who don't have much. So, one thing we need to remember this Thanksgiving is that we need to be mindful of others who have little or nothing to put on their tables. Remember to pray for them daily.

God expects us to be grateful for what we have and to express that gratitude by being kind to others. We need to thank God for our blessings by "paying it forward" and giving to others. What better way to give to others than by praying for them.

We can enjoy our Thanksgiving feast, but at the same time, we need to pray for those who have very little to put on their tables. Remember the less fortunate during this season.

Dear God,

We thank you for being our God and for blessing us so richly. Lord, during this festive time of year, we pray that we will never forget how blessed we are and always stop to give You praise. May everyday be a day of thankfulness, a Thanksgiving Day.

Day 19

"I feel successful when I do my best."

You know, God expects us to do our best in everything we do. Colossians 3:23 says, "Whatever you do, work at it with all your heart, as working for the Lord, not for men."

Whatever we do, God expects us to do our best as if we were doing it for Him, because we really are. We are His witnesses and others look at what we are doing and how we are doing it. If you always do your best, you are being a good representative of the Lord. Others see that and it says a lot about the kind of person you are.

You can feel successful when you always do your best. You can also have the satisfaction that you are doing what the Lord has said for you to do.

So today, whatever you are asked to do, do your very best. It may not be perfect or exactly right, and you may not even like doing it, but if you have done your best, that is all that matters.

Dear God,

Help us to remember today that You expect us to do our best in everything we do—working as unto You.

Thank You for the abilities that You have given each of us and help us to use those abilities to glorify You.

Day 20

"I will turn my negative thoughts into positive ones."

Think of some times when you didn't have the most positive thoughts in your mind. Maybe it was a time when you were having trouble doing something and you were frustrated.

Now look at the trash can in your classroom. What is that can for? It's for trash, isn't it? It has been said that sometimes humans put trash in their own heads by putting negative thoughts in their minds, either about themselves or others.

An example of this might be when we talk to ourselves and say, "I can't do this" or "I'm not good at anything". These thoughts become "trash" for the mind because they get in the way of unique and wonderful characteristics that God has put inside each of us.

However, we can change this if we choose to do so. Someone once used the following illustration: "It's similar to the way we recycle our trash. When we recycle, we take trash and make it into something useful, and it is good for our environment. When you have negative thoughts, you can ask yourself some questions such as, 'Can I change this? If so, how? If not, what can I do to make the most of my situation'"?

Maybe you are having a hard time learning something in one of your classes. Can you change it? What can you say to yourself to make the best of the situation? Maybe you say, "I'll never learn this. Or you ***could*** say, "I really don't like doing this, but I know that if I keep working hard, I will be able to finish this work and I'll eventually get it." Take what started as a negative thought and turn it around into a positive. Recycle your thoughts.

Dear God,

Help us to quickly turn all things around so that we can see the positives and not the negatives.

DECEMBER

Day 1

"God wants us to live in faith."

Someone once described faith as "a special kind of believing". Do you know what believing is? How many of you believe you will have lunch today? Do you believe your mom packed your lunch and put it in your backpack? Do you believe that the lunchroom workers will be serving lunch to the rest of you today in the lunchroom?

So you believe your mom packed your lunch and you believe that the lunchroom workers will be serving lunch today? You believe this because your mom does this everyday, and the lunchroom workers are always in the lunchroom at lunchtime working to get your lunches together.

Well, faith is believing in something you can't necessarily prove. The Bible says that faith is given to us by God. But it is something you may have to practice for it to feel natural (like writing your name in cursive or playing an instrument).

God wants us to have faith. He loves us and He can do all things. This means that God has no problem taking care of us. So we can trust Him. Someone once put it this way, "When we go through our days trusting God and knowing He will help take care of us, that is living in faith."

When we have faith in God, we are blessed. When we trust God (even a little), we find out that He keeps His word. This helps us trust Him even more each day.

The Bible tells us many stories of how people had faith in God and He blessed them for it! Put your faith in God. He will never fail you.

Dear God,

Increase our faith in You daily. Help us to rely on you and to totally give everything to you.

Day 2

"There is a great distance between said and done."
—Puerto Rican Proverb

What exactly does our "Thought for the Day" mean? Well, really, it's very simple. Saying you are going to do something is one thing, but actually doing it, is a totally different thing.

We can put this together in a sentence, but there's a big distance or difference between the two. We can say we will do all kinds of things, ***but*** actually ***doing*** them makes a far greater impact.

Doing the things you say you will do impresses those around you. They start to trust that if you say you will do something, you will take action. That impresses them because you are seen as following through on what you say you will do. You are seen as a trustworthy person. You are putting action to your words.

> Listen to this poem: *There is a great distance between said and done; Almost as far as from the earth to the sun. Words are only words and they can go on all day, But they really mean nothing until you do what you say. So be careful what you say you will do, Because with no action, your words may come back to haunt you (Author Unknown).*

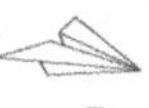

Dear God,

Help us to be people of our word. If we say we are going to do something, help us to do it.

Day 3

"The sleeping fox catches no poultry."
—Ben Franklin

What exactly did Mr. Franklin mean by our Thought for the Day? Well, poultry is chicken and that's what a fox eats mostly. If he's asleep, he will never catch his food. In other words, if he's lazy, he will not eat. That's a big deal!

Laziness has been defined as the failure to do what needs to be done when it needs to be done. It is not doing things at the proper time. It is not making good use of the talents God has given you.

Have you ever thought to yourself when asked to do something, "I shouldn't have to do that!" or, "That's not fair!" Do you think that you have the right to do only what you want?

When your parents ask you to do them a favor or help out around the house, they don't want to give you an extra fifteen minutes to finish that last level of your video game. They need the job done immediately.

Did you know that when you are lazy, you are committing acts of selfishness and you are not being responsible? This is not a good thing.

You shouldn't waste time on things that don't really matter. Take action and spend your time wisely.

How are you spending your time? Are you doing things that make a positive difference? It has been said that today is the first day of the rest of your life. You can choose to make it a wonderful day with God. So rise up and do it!

Dear God,

Help us to be wise as to how we use our time and to never be lazy.

Day 4

"Jesus wants me to obey Him."

We bring joy to the Lord's heart by obeying Him. Let's think about some ways that we can obey the Lord Jesus. The following are great illustrations of this concept once written in a Bible lesson.

"In His word, the Lord tells us things that we should not do. For example, the Bible says, 'Lie not one to another…' God hates lying lips! If we tell lies, we are not obeying the Lord Jesus. So when we speak truth, we obey the Lord and we make Him happy."

The lesson goes on to say that "the Lord not only tells us the things that we should not do, but He also tells us things that we should do. The Bible says to forgive one another as God has forgiven us. This is a very good example of something the Lord says we should "(*Sermons4Kids).*

Did you know that the Lord not only speaks to us in His word, but in our heart. We do not actually hear a voice, but we know, deep down in our heart, when we do something wrong.

Have you ever done something wrong in school? If you have, how did you feel in your heart? You did not feel good because the gentle voice of the Lord Jesus was telling you that it is wrong to do what you did.

When you are in doubt about doing something, ask yourself this question: "Would Jesus want me to do this?" If you think that He does not want you to do it, don't do it!

Today, remember to obey those over you by doing ***what*** you are told, ***when*** you are told to do it, with a good attitude. This will help you have a good day.

Dear God,

Help us to remember that You want us to obey You each and everyday.

Day 5

"As students, we will be peaceful, aware, wise, and safe in the classroom."

What kind of behavior is appropriate in the classroom? Most all of you are great students already, but just so we all can be reminded, let's look at appropriate behavior in the classroom.

"First, what does it mean to ***be peaceful*** in the classroom? It means things like not talking when you are not allowed to talk. Raise your hand quietly, sit quietly, and wait patiently to be called on. That's being peaceful in the classroom.

What is ***being aware*** when in the classroom? Well, simply, it means to follow the teacher's rules. For example, you need to ***listen*** to your teacher explain the procedures for lining up, for writing homework in your notebook, for anything she has you do. ***Listen*** for directions and follow those directions. That's ***being aware***.

How can you ***be wise*** when in the classroom? It means simply to do the best you can do always. Be attentive to your teacher. Do not talk when you are not to be talking. When you have work to do, focus on your work and truly do the best you can do to make it the best it can be. If you do these things, you are ***being wise*** in the classroom.

What does it mean to be ***safe*** when in the classroom? First of all, you need to stay in your seat. Walk into the classroom slowly and quietly, sit down, and stay seated. When you leave the classroom, get up slowly and quietly when dismissed and walk slowly and quietly out of the room. You are being ***safe*** with this behavior" *(Sermons4Kids).*

Most of you have already mastered all of these skills. Thank you, and keep it up!!

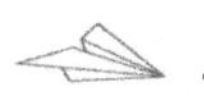

Dear God

Help us to be the students that we need to be each and everyday.

Day 6

"I am like a pencil. I make a mark and have an eraser to correct my mistakes."

Our Thought, and the following illustration, is from the *Sunday School Network*:

"I bought a brand new box of pencils this week. Something funny happened when I took them out of the box. The pencils reminded me of you! You want to know why?

First, they are colored pencils. The colored pencils reminded me of you because your personalities are so colorful. Each of you is different. Because you are different, we can tell you apart from each other.

Do you see what is inside the pencils? Yes. It is lead or the color stuff that makes the pencil work. What is inside leaves a mark on paper, doesn't it? It is the most important part.

Guess what? That lead inside the pencil reminds me of you, too! Because you leave a mark everywhere you go. The words you say can be good words or bad. That leaves a mark. Your actions can make people happy or sad. That leaves a mark. You can help others or hurt others. That leaves a mark. It is what is inside of you that will determine the marks you leave.

See what is on the top of the pencil? It is an eraser. The eraser reminds me of you, too (and of me, too). What do you do with the eraser? When you make a mistake, you can use that eraser to remove it. You and I make mistakes—not just on paper, but in life, too.

We must realize that we make mistakes, but our life eraser is called forgiveness. Jesus will erase our sins! After we erase a mistake on our papers, what do we do? We redo it in the correct way. We ask God to forgive our sins, He does erase them, and we start again."

Dear God,

Help us to never be afraid to correct our mistakes, redo, and "get it right".

Day 7

"I am a child of God. I have feelings. I will work hard to turn my sad feelings to happy ones."

Listen to this poem: *If you chance to meet a frown, Do not let it stay. Quickly turn it upside down, And smile that frown away. No one likes a frowning face. Change it for a smile. Make the world a better place, By smiling all the while (Author Unknown).*

You know, our feelings show in our faces and in our actions. How do you feel when you have a smile on your face? How do you feel when you have a frown on your face?

People can often tell how we feel by looking at our faces. Show your classmates your happy face right now (give time for students to show their classmates their happy faces). Think about it, what makes you feel happy? What makes you feel sad? What makes you feel angry or scared?

It is good to show all of the different feelings we have, but we must show them in the right ways, especially when we are angry. When we are angry, even though we may feel like yelling at someone, or even hitting them, we can learn to show our feelings politely and kindly. When we yell or hit, we only feel angrier, but being kind can help us feel better.

Who can help us feel better when we are sad, angry, or frightened? Those who love us. When we talk to our mom, dad, or others who love us, they can help us understand why we feel like we do. Also, if we pray to our Heavenly Father, He will help us feel better. He will help us know what to do so that we can be happy again. Try it.

Dear God,

Help us to turn our unhappy feelings into happy ones quickly to enjoy life as You want us to.

Day 8

"I believe I can do anything I put my mind to.
I can make a difference in this world."

The following was recently published online about one of our favorite comic strip characters, Snoopy. It relates very well to our Thought for the Day.

"Snoopy is probably one of the most well-known comic strip characters in the world. Of all the Peanuts Gang Characters, Snoopy is probably the one who believes in himself the most.

1. He is liked by the whole gang.
2. He belongs to Charlie Brown who feeds and waters him daily.
3. He plays the saxophone, is "Joe Cool", and is a great happy dancer.
4. He loves impersonating different animals.
5. He has a vivid imagination. He thought he was an astronaut and was the first beagle to land on the moon."

What does it take to believe in yourself enough to say that you can do anything? Well, quite simply, you ***must*** have a relationship with the Lord and let Him guide you daily. Who better to guide you than the Lord? He knows exactly what you need to be doing in the right way. If you allow Him to guide you, He will keep you straight.

Always remember, if God is for you, who can be against you? He always has your back, and will never forsake you.

Keep your faith in Him. He is right by your side everyday, in every situation.

When you start to see how God is helping you through different things, you will slowly gain the confidence you need to believe in yourself. He created you. You can do anything you put your mind to ***if*** God is in the middle of it! God will help you make a difference!

Dear God,

Help us to believe in ourselves and to daily keep our eyes on you.

Day 9

"When I share what I have with others, I have more of it."

What if, when you go to lunch today, you see that the person sitting next to you doesn't have anything to eat. What might you do? You can share your food, can't you? It's good to share.

Chances are that all of us have shared something with someone else sometime in our lives. Likewise, we have all probably received something that someone else has shared with us.

Some people are very good at sharing. Many of you have shared your toys, clothes, food, and other things. All of you are especially good at sharing smiles and kind words and even hugs.

The believers in the early church shared everything they had. People then, who owned land or houses, sold them and brought the money to the apostles to give to others in need.

The early believers were so good at sharing what they had that there wasn't a needy person among them. Because everybody shared, everyone had what was needed. If we ask, God will help us also become sharing people. And, like many things we do, the more we practice sharing, the better we become at it, and the more God will bless us.

So, during this holiday season, remember to practice sharing and see how good you become at it. Don't forget to ask God to help you.

Dear God,

Thank you for all that you have given us. Teach us to be generous with all the gifts that you have blessed us with. Help us, daily, to share what we have with others.

Day 10

"Since I tell the truth, my friends trust me."

It is important to tell the truth, isn't it? First of all, it is important because that is what God expects us to do. However, have you ever thought about how difficult things can become for you if you don't tell the truth?

It seems more times than not, if you don't tell the truth the first time, you have to keep on covering up things to cover the lie you told. You just tend to get yourself into more and more trouble.

In addition, your friends start to question if you are ever telling them the truth if they have found you not being honest with them to begin with. It is a very difficult situation to find yourself in.

> Listen to this short poem about telling the truth: *I will tell the truth always, Even if it's hard. I will use my tongue for good, And daily stay on guard. For God expects truth from me, No matter where I am. So my friends will always know, That on God's word I stand (Author Unknown).*

So remember, in order for your friends to trust you, it is important to always tell the truth. God will be smiling down upon you when you do this.

Dear God,

Help us to always speak the truth, no matter how hard it is, realizing that this is what You expect of us. May we be good examples for others each and everyday of our lives.

Day 11

"Actions speak louder than words."

This is a very familiar phrase and many of you may have heard this many times. Have you ever really thought about the fact that actions ***do*** speak louder than words. People can say anything, but when what they say and what they do don't match up, it is easy to judge them by what is done instead of by what is said.

For instance, if a classmate says, "We should all be obedient to our teacher today", but then that classmate is the first one to disobey the teacher with his/her actions, then what do we remember the most? Do we remember what they said or what they did? Obviously, we remember what they did the most.

Have you ever heard the phrase: "...saying one thing and doing another"? Well, this is a prime example of what we are discussing now.

So remember: What you do is what people will remember much more than the things you say. Make sure your words and your actions are positive and that they match up. If they match up, then they will have equal value.

Dear God,

Help us to take positive action on things and to make sure what we do matches what we say.

Day 12

"If there are things about myself that I don't like, I can change them if I want to. I just need to choose to change them."

We all have things about ourselves that we don't like, don't we? Maybe it is that we don't study enough, or we don't obey our authority figures, or maybe we skip our chores. There can be a lot of things that we would like to change.

But the first step in changing is that you must first choose to change. You don't have to live with those things that you don't like—you just have to make up your mind that you are going to correct those things you dislike so much, and then get to it, one step at a time.

Think about the things that you would like to change; you might even write them down. Then start working on those areas one little bit at a time. Day by day, as you work to improve those things, you will see that a change is taking place.

Soon you will see that you have it right where you want it. So remember, change is possible. Instead of giving in to those negative things you don't like about yourself, make up your mind that you are going to work on changing those negatives to positives. With God's help, all things are possible.

Dear God,

If we see negative things in ourselves that need to be changed, give us the strength and assistance to work on changing them. Help us to remember that nothing is impossible with you.

Day 13

"When I am not happy, I can always think of the good things I have in life and it makes me feel better."

There are times when all of us feel a bit unhappy. That's a part of life. However, there is a very simple thing we can do to help us feel better. Sometimes if we sit down and just list in our heads all the good things we have, that can easily make us feel better when we feel a bit sad.

Let's just take a few minutes to list some of your wonderful blessings. This way, you can think back upon them when you need to be reminded of the good things in your life:

1. One of your greatest blessings is your school. You have a school where you can learn about God and praise Him daily while learning the things you need to learn.
2. You have the blessing of having teachers and staff members who love you and who work extremely hard to make sure you are getting what you need to get daily.
3. You have your families who work hard, support you, and love you unconditionally.
4. Even though you may not see this as a blessing, you each are blessed to be doing all the hard work in your classrooms daily. You are blessed to have your studies, as this is preparing you for your future.
5. You have the blessing of prayer in that you can take your concerns and your requests to the Lord and feel confident that He will take care of you.

We could probably go on and on, but the next time you start to feel sad, stop and think about some of these things you are blessed with. If you do, you won't be sad for long.

Dear God,

Help us to quickly focus on our many blessings when we start to feel sad, and to remember You.

Day 14
Christmas

"Glory to God in the highest."

Christmas is such a special time of year. It is the time when we celebrate the birth of Christ. Our Thought for the Day comes from the very first Christmas.

Christmas is almost here this year. We have Christmas every year to celebrate that Jesus, the Savior, was born. Let's talk about the very first Christmas.

The first Christmas, Mary and Joseph had traveled to Bethlehem and, as you know, there was no room for them in the inn, but they finally found a place to stay in a stable. Baby Jesus was born while they were there.

When a new baby is born, parents often call and let all their friends know about the birth. Since God is Jesus' Father, He wanted the whole world to know that His one and only Son had been born in Bethlehem. How did he let everyone know? He sent angels to visit the shepherds who were watching their sheep. The angels talked to the shepherds. They announced the birth of Jesus and then, all of a sudden, the sky was full of angels singing praises to God. They sang, "Glory to God in the highest, and on earth, peace, good will toward men."

The shepherds went to Bethlehem to see the Savior, worship Him, and praise God. So we, likewise, need to remember to praise God this Christmas too. Glory to God in the highest!

Dear God,

Thank you for sending Baby Jesus. Thank you that He is Your Son and our Savior.

Thank you for Christmas.

Day 15
Christmas

"And she gave birth to her firstborn, a son. She wrapped Him in cloths and placed Him in a manger, because there was no room for them in the inn."
—Luke 2:7

It's almost here! We are about to start our Christmas holiday. Don't you just love Christmas? What do you like best about Christmas? Is it the Christmas tree, Christmas dinner, all of the parties or visiting with family and friends? What about the presents?

Hmmm…Can you think of anything we have left out? Oh, yes! It's someone's birthday, isn't it? Whose birthday is it? That's right. It is

Jesus' birthday. You know, sometimes we get so caught up in all of the decorations, parties, and presents that we miss the Real Christmas.

Someone once wrote a story to illustrate this point very well:

"There once was a little boy who had always wanted to go to a circus. One day he was walking down the street when he saw a poster in a store window. The poster said that a circus was coming to town and that a ticket to the circus cost one dollar. The boy ran home and asked his father if he would give him a dollar to go to the circus on Saturday.

His father told him that if he would work hard and get all of his chores done, he would give him a dollar to go to the circus. Saturday morning came and the boy got up early and did all of his chores. His father gave him a dollar and the boy headed into town filled with excitement about seeing wild animals, trapeze artists, and all of the things that come with a circus.

Since he arrived in town so early, he was on the front row when the circus parade started down the main street of town. The boy was thrilled when the animals and the other circus acts paraded by.

At the end of the parade came the clowns and following the clowns was the ringmaster. When the ringmaster passed by where he was standing, the boy ran out into the street, took his folded dollar bill from his pocket, and handed it to the ringmaster.

"Thanks, Mister," said the boy, "That was a great circus." Then he turned around and walked home. He never knew what he had missed. He thought he had been to the circus, but he had only been to the parade" (Sermons4Kids).

If we are not careful, we can get so caught up in the celebration that we miss the Real Christmas—the birthday of our Savior, Jesus.

Dear God,

We pray that we won't get so caught up in the celebration that we miss the Real Christmas.

JANUARY

Day 1

"Hold fast to dreams, for if dreams die, you will truly never be able to do any of those things because you will be like a broken-winged bird that cannot fly."
—Langston Hughes

Welcome back, everyone! Hopefully, you each had a wonderful holiday and were truly blessed by your time off and your time to focus on the birth of Christ.

You know, the New Year is usually the time when people start thinking about what they are going to be doing differently in the future to make things better. Sometimes people start to look way ahead and think about what they want to work toward. We call that a "dream" that we have—not the type you have when you sleep, but a dream, as in, what you imagine you'd like to do; what you consider might be a possibility for you to do in the future. You might hear someone say, "I have a dream to be…"

So, *Hold fast to your dreams* means to hold fast to what you imagine you can do, hope to do, or may be able to do. *For if dreams die*, means if you quit thinking you can do those things then you will never be able to do them.

You must continue to believe that you can accomplish your dreams, with God's help, of course. With God on your side, you can accomplish anything!

So with the beginning of this New Year, remember, with the Lord all things are possible. You never know what great things you can accomplish!

Dear God,

Help us to focus on those things that You have planned for us and help us to dream big—knowing that if it is in Your plan, we will be successful in accomplishing our dreams.

Day 2

"Anything you learn becomes your wealth, a wealth that cannot be taken away from you; whether you learn it in a building called school or in the school of life. To learn something new is a timeless pleasure and a valuable treasure."

—C. JoyBell C.

You know, you can ***buy*** lots of different things, and many of those things become very valuable to you. Nevertheless, any of those things can be taken away from you at any given time.

However, anything you learn and put in your mind can never be taken away from you—it will always be there with you. That's why it's so important to learn as much as you can because you are adding to your wealth of knowledge and you will always have it.

So as you are going through your day today, remember that everything you are learning is adding to the treasure in your mind. It can never be taken away from you. Be thankful that you have the ability to learn each day.

You have a valuable treasure that will never go away. Be thankful for it!

Dear God,

Help us to be excited about learning and to remember that we should always do our best to add to our wealth of knowledge.

Day 3

"The bird has a nest, a spider has a web, man has friendship."
—William Blake

It is likely that you are looking at each other right now saying, "What in the world does that mean? That makes no sense." What exactly does our Thought for the Day mean? Well, the bird lives in a nest and the spider lives in a web. Those are their homes.

Mr. Blake is saying that friendship is kind of like a home for man. Home is a place where we are safe; it's a place where we can be ourselves; it's a place where we are taken care of, and where we are sheltered.

The same is true of our friendships. Think about it—we feel safe with our friends, we are accepted by them, and we just feel at home with them. So when Mr. Blake says man has friendship, he means that man sees his friends in much the same way as we see our homes—we are safe with our friends.

Listen to the following poem about friendship:

A friend is someone we turn to, When our spirits need a lift. A friend is someone we treasure, For our friendship is a gift. A friend is someone who fills our lives, With beauty, joy, and grace, And makes the world we live in, A better and happier place (kidsgen.com).

So be a friend to others and be thankful for the friends you have. God has given them to you to be a blessing—appreciate this blessing.

Dear God,

Thank you for the gift of friendship. Lord, help us appreciate the friends we have.

Day 4

"A man of words and not of deeds is like a garden full of weeds."

—Percy B. Green

What does our Thought for the Day mean? It means that if you just talk all the time about what you are going to do, but you don't do anything, it is like a garden where no flowers grow, and weeds take over. In other words, talking only, and not acting, accomplishes nothing.

For example, let's say that you tell your parents, students, that you are going to start cleaning your room everyday, and you ***say that everyday***, but you never do it. Then you are just talking, not acting.

According to our Thought, ***your words have the possibility of producing a great thing***—just like the garden. However, if you do nothing, then nothing happens and, just like in the garden, the weeds grow instead of flowers.

We need to put actions to our words and avoid becoming like "a garden full of weeds"; something that could be beautiful, but turns into something not so nice. People then start to distrust what you say and they don't believe you anymore.

If you say you are going to do something, do it! Don't let the weeds grow in the garden. Make it something beautiful!

Dear God,

Help us to be people of our word. Lord, if we say we are going to do something, help us to hold firm to what we say we are going to do and do it!

Day 5

"If any of you lacks wisdom, he should ask God, who gives generously to all without finding fault, and it will be given to him."

—James 1:5

What is wisdom? Wisdom means having the ability to know what is right. Now, there are two kinds of wisdom: man's wisdom and God's wisdom.

We, as humans, often think that wisdom is being smart. People often feel that wisdom is having a successful life. However, there is more to wisdom than that. There is Godly wisdom, which is knowing God, and what His words tell us, as far as how to live a life that pleases Him. Having God's wisdom brings true peace and satisfaction. Godly wisdom is what we should strive to have.

Solomon, in the Bible, was a very wise man. King David, his father, had given his son some advice before he was king. He instructed him to acknowledge God and serve Him with His whole heart. That is what Solomon did. He went on to be a very wise King.

It is a gift to have people in our life who teach us to love and obey God. Just like Solomon, it is a blessing to be obedient to what our parents and family members have taught us.

We will probably never be a king as Solomon was, but as God's children, the work that God has called us to do is just as important. We need Godly wisdom to lead a life that pleases God. We want to be examples to lead others to Jesus. If we ask God for wisdom, we can make wise decisions and help others to see Jesus in our lives.

Dear God,

Help us to always seek Godly wisdom rather than man's wisdom.

Day 6

"Self-motivation, or making yourself want to do something, is very important. It comes from a desire to achieve something and the belief that we are capable of doing it without getting discouraged."
—Anonymous

Self-motivation means simply that you feel the need or desire to do something and you take action. Now, think about that. What do you want to do this school year? What is your goal? For example: Maybe you want to make the Honor Roll, or maybe you want to read more books, or perhaps, you want to have the highest average in one of your classroom subjects.

You have to have a plan. Break your ***big*** goal into smaller steps that you can meet each week or each day. Maybe you can decide how many books you want to read in one week and do that. Eventually they start to accumulate. Maybe you want to make the highest average in your math class. Start with the first test and make the best grade you can make, and then go to the next.

Get rid of thoughts and ideas that might get in your way. Words like "can't" can really bring you down and hinder you in achieving your goal. Believe in yourself and in God's power to help you accomplish your goal.

After you have reached your goal, think about how you feel now that you have accomplished something so important to you. Realize we used the word ***after*** you have reached your goal. You see, you ***can*** reach your goal, but you have to want to reach your goal, and not get discouraged—that's self-motivation.

Dear God,

Help us to have the desire to always do our best and to accomplish those things we have ahead of us. Help us to want to accomplish those tasks and to not get discouraged in doing so.

Day 7

"Every time I look in the mirror, I say something good to that person."

Have you ever talked to yourself while looking in a mirror? Have you ever said out loud, while looking in the mirror, "I am going to do great on my math test today!" or, "I am a really nice friend." or, maybe you just said something that helped you feel good about yourself.

It could be that some of you want to laugh right now, and that is understandable. It probably seems silly to look in the mirror and just talk. However, it is so important for us to learn to respect ourselves, just like you've learned to respect everyone else in the school. You are just as important as they are.

We talk about respect so much, and that is so important. But what does it mean to respect yourself? It means really to see the good inside of yourself—the part the mirror doesn't show.

God made all of us special and He has plans to use the good in each of us for His glory.

Listen to this short poem:

As I look into the mirror, What do I really see? Am I looking at only the outside, Or deep inside of me? I see a positive, friendly person,

Who strives to lend a hand, And goes the extra mile, Just to help those I can. I don't always get everything right, But I pick myself up and move on, Because I am God's child, created by Him, And with Him, the battle is won. Yes, my reflection in the mirror shows the image others see, But with God's help daily, I hope to show others The beauty deep inside of me.

Dear God,

Help us to respect all those we come in contact with today, and to respect ourselves as well.

Day 8

"I have the courage to stand up for those who are being picked on by others. I am helpful to those who do not have the courage to stand up for themselves."

What does courage mean? It means facing your fears with confidence—being brave. It means doing the right thing, even if it is difficult.

What are some ways you can show courage? Someone once put it into three quick steps: "Do the right thing even if others are not; Bravely deal with daily struggles; and, Don't give in to negative classmate pressure." In other words, don't give in to what your classmates are doing that is wrong.

Let's say that you see your friend being made fun of and being laughed at by others. What do you do? Do you start doing the same thing that the others are doing or do you courageously take a stand and speak up for your friend?

Well, obviously, all of you know what God expects you to do. He expects you to stand up against the things that are not right. Each time someone stands up against this behavior, it helps put an end to it.

If you see someone doing this to someone else, tell them to stop what they are doing and then go tell an adult. Don't give in to this negative behavior.

It takes courage to do the right thing. Stand up for what is right, even if you stand alone because you are not really standing alone. God is right beside you.

Dear God,

Help us to be courageous and to do the right thing when we see our friends being picked on or made fun of. Help us to stand up for them and to do what is right.

Day 9

"I care about those who take care of our school so I will pick up my trash and make sure I don't leave things lying around. I will strive hard to help out where I can."

You know, there is a lot of hard work that goes into keeping our building clean and ready for us to have classes each day. And just like your parents appreciate you cleaning up after yourself at home, those who have the responsibility for cleaning our building appreciate all the help you can give them as well.

It's really very simple. If you have trash, throw it in the trash can. Don't leave it lying around. If you see trash, even if it isn't yours, pick it up and throw it away.

If you go into the bathroom, don't leave water on the counter. Wipe it up. Don't leave paper towels in the floor. Pick them up.

Make sure you pick up all your things each day as you leave the area that you are in. Lastly, help keep your classrooms nice and neat as well.

Each of us can make a huge difference just by doing our part to clean up where we can. And you know what? You will probably feel really good about yourself after you do that. Try it.

Dear God,

Help us to be respectful of those who keep our school clean and to help them out by picking up our trash, and cleaning up after ourselves.

Day 10

"As you do your work today, know that God is with you.
As you go to sleep tonight, know that God is watching over you."

Isn't this a wonderful Thought for the Day? Isn't it great to think each day, "God is right beside me throughout the day, no matter what I am doing"? He is like this friend walking beside you, guiding and directing you through every moment of your life.

And at night, isn't it awesome that God never sleeps? He is watching over you as you sleep soundly. You don't have to worry that He won't take care of you, even as you sleep. If something is bothering you, give it all to Him and sleep soundly because He is awake and will take care of you.

Listen to this short poem:

God walks by our side each day, Saying, "Child you need to get out of my way". Allow Me to guide, guard, and direct you, And to hold your hand until the struggle you pass through. And then, at night, when you close your eyes in sleep, Hand over your problems and give them to Me. Never worry about my bedtime, Because I never sleep nor close my eyes. I watch over you each moment with care, And smile, with love, when you end your day in prayer (Author Unknown).

Dear God,

Help us to remember today that You are with us, constantly helping us and guiding us throughout the day. Help us to rely on Your guidance and may we always do what You would have us do.

Day 11

"I appreciate my teachers for teaching me what they know and for doing the best they can to help me grow."

Have you ever thought about how much your teachers do for you and how much they care for you? Sometimes we don't take the time to think about that, do we?

There are many times when you are at home on the weekends having fun, and your teachers are here at the school working. Did you know that?

They are in your classrooms getting things ready for the next day's lesson. They are writing the assignments on the boards, running off copies on the copy machine, grading your papers and all kinds of other things.

They are taking their time when school is not in session to do the things they need to do to get ready to teach you the next day. They want to make sure they are doing it to the best of their ability so that they can give you what you need to have and so they can help you grow.

Now, that's special, isn't it? They don't have to do that, but they want to do that because they love you and they love the Lord. They want to do all things according to the way that He would have them do it.

So today, why not say thank you to your teachers to let them know that you appreciate all they do for you. They are a very special group.

Dear God,

We thank you for our special teachers and for all they do for us and for this school. Help us to show them how much they are loved and appreciated.

Day 12

"If I stop, think, and pray before I do things, I know I will do the right thing. God has told us what the right things are in the Bible. I only need to follow what He says."

Have you ever done something or made a decision about something quickly without thinking? All of us have, haven't we? And most of the time, when we do something without thinking and praying about it, it usually doesn't turn out the way it needs to.

Rather than do things immediately, we need to stop and think about whether what we make the decision to do, or not do, will have consequences. We need to take time to pray to God to get His wisdom on what we should or should not be doing. Wouldn't you rather be sure that your actions will be honorable ones rather than ones that dishonor the Lord?

Nothing is so important that a decision must be made without giving it any thought or time in prayer. Talk to God, your friend, before you make any decision. He's got your back!

Dear God,

Help us to get in the habit of asking for Your wisdom and direction before making any decisions. Help us to never rely upon ourselves, but to rely totally upon You for all things.

Day 13

"Success comes from knowing that you did your best
to become the best that you are capable of becoming."
—John Wooden

Now, what exactly do we mean by the word, success? Someone once wrote the following poem about the meaning of success:

Success isn't having trophies or toys, It isn't a medal or friends of your choice, What is success? That's easy to see, It's trying to be the best you can be (Author Unknown)!

Success is trying to be the best you can be in all the different areas of your life! And you know, that's what God expects of us, too.

There is a lot involved in trying to be the best you can be. You must be a hard worker who does every job, even those that are difficult, to the very best of your ability. You must get in the habit of working hard, even on difficult things.

You need to be someone others can count on, you need to be honest, you need to be cooperative (that means that you need to work well with others), and you definitely need to be determined (that means that you have a strong feeling that you are going to do something, and that you will not allow anyone or anything to stop you—even failure). You will keep trying.

Being successful comes down to being the best you can be in every area of your life. And truly, that is what God expects of each of us everyday. So let's all strive for success today!

Dear God,

Help us strive for success by being the best we can be for You.

Day 14

"Make an effort everyday to feel good
about who you are and what you can be."

It is so important for you to love yourself. When we say you need to love yourself that means that you need to appreciate the person God has made you to be. Be thankful for you!

In our world today, people feel loving themselves means to be stuck-up, and to think that you are better than everyone else, whereas God's way of having you love yourself is very different. It is based on being humble and thankful for what He has blessed you with.

We are created in God's image and whenever you don't like yourself, you're actually looking down on something that God has made. That's quite a thought, isn't it? Are we saying that God made something bad when He made us? God made us all "in His own image" and that can't be bad.

If God created you in His image, then you are saying that ***His*** image is not a good one if you look down on yourself. ***Never, never, never*** look down on yourself because ***God*** made you and He makes only wonderful, great things.

Don't let those bad thoughts creep into your head. Make an effort everyday to feel good about who you are and what you can be because your Creator is perfect and He doesn't make mistakes.

Dear God,

Thank you for making us in Your unique image. We know that You make everything awesome and we are Your creation. That makes us very special.

Day 15

"If something is bothering me, I will tell my mom and dad because they love me and they want to help me feel better."

Have you ever had something bothering you, but you just kept it to yourself and didn't tell anyone about your feelings? What usually happens when you don't talk about something that's bothering you? It just seems to bother you more.

It is always a good idea to talk about things that trouble you, and who better to talk to than your parents? Your parents love you so much. The only one who loves you more than your parents is God. They want what is best for you and sometimes, in order to feel better, it is as simple as just talking about your feelings.

So if you find yourself sad or bothered by something, instead of keeping it to yourself, talk to your parents. It won't be long before you will feel much better.

Listen to this short poem:

Goodness, I am sad today. It makes me want to cry, And pout, and whine, and whimper, And sniffle, sob and sigh. Instead I use my words, To tell my loved ones why (Author Unknown).

Remember, always talk to your parents and to God about anything. You will find that you'll feel much better if you do.

Dear God,

When we find ourselves bothered by something, give us the courage to talk about it and to pray about it because we know that this will always make us feel better.

Day 16

"I am being punctual when I am on time and do not keep people waiting."

What does it mean to be punctual? It simply means "on time". Now how does that relate to each of you? You are probably saying, "Well, I don't drive so if I'm late to school, it's someone else who is driving."

That's true, however, sometimes you can still be the reason that you are late. Maybe you didn't get dressed when you were supposed to, or you took longer getting up out of bed than you needed to. All of those things can contribute to you not being on time or punctual.

When you are being dropped off in the morning, does it take you too long to get your things together to get out of the car? If so, you need to have everything right with you and ready to go so you won't be holding others up. In the afternoon, when your parents are picking you up, again, you need to be ready to go when they get here. You know, when you are not being punctual, you are not only holding up your parent, but all the rest of the cars behind your parent who are waiting as well.

All of this comes under the category of being punctual. You need to be on time for everything you do. Don't wait to the last minute to do something. Others are depending on you, so be responsible—be punctual—be on time.

Dear God,

Help us to stay focused and attentive to what we need to be doing. Help us remember how important it is to be punctual because when we're not, we are causing others problems as well. Help us to be responsible people.

Day 17

"I follow the rules and try to make my school a better place."

Our school is great, isn't it? We have a great place that we come to everyday. When you enter the building, you can feel the love that everyone has for you and for each other. We have the opportunity to learn in a caring environment and to put God in the middle of everything we do.

We truly need to appreciate the good things we have here. And one reason our school is such a good one is because you all follow the rules the way the Lord wants you to.

When people don't follow the rules, there is no order and there is confusion. Rules are important and they have a purpose.

We each want all of you students to know how much we appreciate the fact that you do follow the rules. You make our already great school, even better. Keep it up!

Dear God,

We want to thank you for these great students that we have here in our school. They are such a blessing to us and we look forward to seeing the wonderful impact they are going to have on others in the future.

Day 18

"The greatest treasures of your life are the people you love and who love you."

A treasure is something considered especially precious or valuable. You know, when you think about having treasures here on earth, what better treasure can you have than the treasure of those people you love and care for and who love and care for you.

Your parents, your grandparents, your uncles, your aunts, your other family members, and your dear friends are true treasures here on earth. You can count on them and rely on them to care for you and to do what is best for you.

Sometimes when we think of treasures, we think of something kept in a treasure chest because it is so valuable that we don't want to take the chance of it being spoiled or "messed up". We want to protect those treasures.

Well, God's protection is like that treasure chest. He takes care of all of us, and that includes the people we hold most dear.

We are truly rich when we look at all the wonderful family members and friends we have been given. They are the best treasures here on earth that we could ever have. Don't take them for granted. Tell them how special they are to you.

Dear God,

Thank you for those we love and for those who love us back. What true blessings they are. Help us to remember how blessed we are.

Day 19

"Sharing with others makes me feel good and makes them feel good too. It is what God wants me to do."

All of you know that God has given us so much, and because He has given us so much, there is joy in sharing with others. It makes us feel really good inside when we share what we have with others. We see the smile it puts on their face and it automatically puts one on our face too.

You know, Jesus is happy when we give, even a little. We need to give to others out of love, not to impress anyone.

When your parents give to those in need, those they have shared with, can buy food, pay for a place to live, buy blankets—and one day, maybe they can share with others also. That is what God wants.

Continue to share on a daily basis—God is pleased with that. Have a sharing spirit everyday. God takes our gifts, even something as small as a pencil shared with a friend, and makes them count in big ways!

Dear God,

Help us to be mindful of those who don't have as much as we do and who just need others around them with a sharing spirit. Help us to be kind and generous and always willing to lend a hand to help.

Day 20

"I will work hard everyday to never intentionally do or say anything to hurt someone else."

Have you ever heard any of your classmates tease others or use words that put someone down or that made them feel lonely or unhappy? I am sure that all of us can say that we have heard this happen at one time or another.

You know, our words and actions are important and have power. Our words and actions matter.

When you hear unkind words used to put down others, have you ever thought about how ***you*** would feel if those words were said to you? Would you want to come back to school? Would you feel like doing your best work? Do hurtful words and actions help others? Of course not. All of you know the answer to these questions.

All of you know the importance of being kind to your friends, but it never hurts any of us to be reminded that we need to be very careful not to say or do anything that could, in any way, hurt anyone else. God expects better of us.

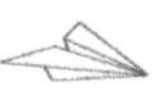

Dear God,

We pray that we will always honor you in all things, especially in our words and actions. Help us to be the good examples that we need to be.

Day 21

"Rules are extremely important and they guide most of our actions with other people each day. Without them, there would be no order."

There are rules in place all around us, aren't there? You have rules in your classroom, rules on the playground, and rules at home too, don't you?

You know, for you older students, you have learned about the rules of our country and how our leaders go about making and putting in place rules to help our country run more smoothly.

Rules are an important part of all of our lives. If you play a game and you don't have rules to follow, how do you know what to do? If you have no rules, there is ***no order*** and then everything is out-of-control.

All of you are to be commended for how well, overall, you follow the rules our school has, and the rules your teacher has in the classroom. There is a good reason you need to continue to do that daily and that is because God is a God of order and rules help us keep order in our lives.

Rules are in place for a reason.

Dear God,

Help us to do the right thing; to make good choices, and to follow those rules that have been put in place.

Day 22

"Whatever you do, work at it with all your heart, as working for the Lord, not for human masters."
—(Col. 3:23)

This verse reminds us of the character trait of diligence. What does it mean to be diligent? It means to steadily keep doing what you are doing, even if it's a bit difficult. It means to constantly keep working at a job in an effort to complete it successfully. It means not being lazy.

We need to truly work to be diligent in all we do. We need to practice diligence everyday. Someone once posted the following to help us practice diligence:

1. I will finish my projects.
2. I will do a job right.
3. I will follow instructions.
4. I will concentrate on my work.
5. I will not be lazy.

When we are diligent, we please God, we are thoughtful and considerate of others, we meet deadlines, and we work well with others" *(Character Trait Poster)*. Those are very positive things, aren't they?

If we work to be diligent, God will be pleased with our efforts. "Whatever you do, work at it with all your heart, as working for the Lord."

Dear God,

Thank you for giving us the ability to do the work ahead of us well. Help us to strive to be diligent people; people who do our jobs to the best of our ability, doing it as unto You. Remind us, Lord, when we start to "take the easy way out" that You expect our best always.

FEBRUARY

Day 1

"I am unique and special, created by God for a purpose. There is no one else like me in the entire world. I do not have to wear certain things, dress a certain way, or do anything in particular to be unique. If I am myself, that is my uniqueness."

Psalm 139:14 says, "I will praise you, for I am fearfully and wonderfully made." In the Hebrew text, the word, *wonderfully*, means: unique, set apart, uniquely marvelous.

God is the artist who created each of us with much love. According to the scripture, each of us truly is a masterpiece and God cares for, and loves us, with a love that is limitless.

We have often heard it said that we are essentially a genuine and unique work of art produced by God Himself. Our lives are meant to reflect the beauty of God's love.

Did you know that when God created us to be unique individuals He gave us each certain characteristics that only we have? Each of us has been given traits that are unique to us for a purpose.

It has been said many times that God wants us to reflect the beauty of His love and to do that with the unique characteristics He has given us. He has a purpose for each of our lives and He expects us to use our uniqueness to fulfill His purpose.

So remember, you simply need to be yourself because you are already unique and special, created by God for a purpose.

Dear God,

Thank You for creating us each uniquely. Help us to remember that You think each of us is very special and You have a plan for each one of us.

Day 2

"Everyone has the same 24 hours a day. Some people use them wisely and others waste their time. I will learn to use my time wisely, and when I do, I will find the time to do more of the things I want to do."

This thought is probably more for you older students because as you get older, you see how important it is to manage your time. What does it mean when we say, "manage your time"?

By "manage your time", we mean simply to do the things you need to do, when you need to do them, and get them done. Plan ahead what tasks you will do, and when you will do them.

Have you ever found at home, when your parents give you things to do, that after you get them done, you have more time to do what ***you*** want? Isn't that a good feeling?

This is essentially a good rule to follow: get the things done that need to be done and then you will have time left for the fun things. When you have completed your chores, you will enjoy your fun things more too!

Listen to this short poem:

Twenty-four hours, that's all there is, In one complete day. Time is short when there is much to do, So we must do our work before play. We work hard on the chores before us, Homework, household chores, and other tasks, So we can have extra time when finished, To do the fun things when someone asks (Author Unknown).

Dear God,

Help us to use our time wisely. Help us to always attend to our work and other jobs first, so that we can get the important things done in order to have more time to do the things we want to do.

Day 3

"There are so many different places in the world. People in other countries do things in a very different way. God made this world

as a world of differences—many people, from many countries, doing things differently. Learning about those differences is fun."

You know, there are many different countries in our world, aren't there? It is likely that some of you older students have been studying about some of them.

There are many people who speak different languages and who do things much differently than we do them. It is exciting to learn about other places and how the people there do, maybe the same things we do, but how they do them in such a different way.

God made all of us uniquely and learning about different countries, languages, customs and traditions should be something we all enjoy. These are people just like us, but they have different ways of doing commonplace things.

So, in your classrooms, as you study about different countries and languages, remember that God made those people too and we should be interested in learning about all the things that make them so unique to us.

Dear God,

Help us be excited about learning today. Help us realize that you have made us all different for a reason and that we should enjoy learning about those differences.

Day 4

"Correctly practicing something creates success. If I continue to practice something successfully, and do it enough, I can accomplish

almost anything I want. Successful people were not born that way. They practiced success until they accomplished it."

There is a common saying, "Practice makes perfect." However, practice doesn't make perfect if you are practicing something the wrong way. It would, perhaps, be more accurate to say, "Practice makes permanent."

Our Thought for Today focuses on doing something the right way and practicing it enough that you become successful at it. You keep trying over and over until you get it.

Think about something that when you first started doing it, it was hard for you to do. However, after you started practicing it more and more, it got easier and easier until you finally got really good at it.

Think about the first time you tried to ride a bicycle. You probably struggled with it at first, but the more you did it, the better you got, until it became a very natural thing to do.

In order to do something well, you must keep practicing it. So don't get discouraged if you try something and you aren't good at it at first —keep trying, keep practicing—you'll be amazed at what practice will do for you.

Dear God,

Help us to be the good examples that You want us to be and to not give up when things get hard. Help us to continue to strive to be the best we can be, knowing that if we do our part, You will be right there to help us.

Day 5

"I think before I act. How I act affects how others treat me."

As all of you know, it is very important for us to stop and think before we do something. We need to think about how our actions will affect others before we act.

You might want to use what someone published as the ***Stop**, **Think**, **Decide** **Method*** before you act. First, you ***Stop***. Don't do anything immediately. Second, you need to ***Think***. Spend some time thinking about how you would feel if your action was done to you. Third, ***Decide*** whether your action is a positive or a negative one and whether God would be pleased with you if you act on it.

This short poem just about sums it up:

> *I think before I act, And take my time before I speak. I ask myself if what I plan to do, Will make someone smile or weep. I stop, think, and decide, Before I move into action, Will what I do bring a smile, Or cause a negative reaction? I will be slow to move and quick to think, Because I want to make the right choice. I will think before I act, And listen to God's small inner voice.*

Dear God,

Help us, Lord, to think before we act so that we can be good examples for You always.

Day 6

"God gives us so much. We should never forget to give Him thanks for all He does for us."

What do you say when someone gives you something special? What do you say when someone does something for you that makes you feel happy? What do you say when someone does something to show they love you?

Did you ever forget to say thank you? If this happened, one of your parents probably said, “What do you say?” to remind you to say thank you.

Do you like to be thanked when you take the time to do something nice for someone? How would you feel if you took a long time making something for someone and when you gave it to them, they didn’t even say thank you?

Why should we say thank you? Of course, to show the person who did something nice for us that we appreciate it.

Do you think Jesus likes to be thanked when He does something nice for us? Of course He does.

Sometimes we don’t even think about all the good things that God gives us. Sometimes we don’t even realize everything that God has given us or how important they are until something happens. For example, we don’t realize how important it is to have a healthy body until we get sick. We should thank God for keeping us healthy.

God has given us so much. We should never forget to thank Him for all He does for us.

Dear God,

Thank you for everything You have given us. We are so blessed to have so much. You are such a good God to bless us so richly. Help us to never take all of these blessings for granted.

Day 7

"Before you start talking about another person's faults, you need to take time to count to ten—and list ten of your own."

Sometimes it's really easy to look only at other people's faults, isn't it? We find things that we want to criticize about them—never really looking at our own weaknesses.

You know, no one is perfect—if we were, we wouldn't be living here on earth. Everyone has faults, and unfortunately, we all get tempted to talk about someone else's faults.

So, according to our Thought for the Day, the next time you start to talk about someone else's faults, start listing your own faults. That will probably help you see that we have no right to criticize anyone else.

Dear God,

Make us aware of the fact that no one is perfect and we all have faults. Help us to stop and focus on our own faults when we get tempted to start talking about others' faults. Help us to remember that we are all imperfect human beings, and truly, without You, we would be nothing.

Day 8

"I treat others the way I want them to treat me. If I want people to help me, I help others. If I want them to encourage me, I encourage others. If I want them to love me, I love others."

Does this Thought of the Day sound familiar to you? It is familiar to you because this is based on the Bible verse found in Luke 6:31: "Do unto others as you would have them do unto you." We often refer to this as The Golden Rule.

It makes perfect sense, doesn't it? We should treat other people the way we want to be treated. It seems very simple, and yet, sometimes, it's a very difficult thing for us to do.

We need to constantly remind ourselves that this is what God expects us to do. If we do this, we will be happier people for it.

In order to do this, we must have feelings of kindness for others. What we think determines what we do. When our feelings are based upon kind thoughts, we will act with love and respect toward others. In addition, we will be pleasing God in the way we treat others.

Dear God,

Help us each to remember to treat others the way we, ourselves, want to be treated. Help us to look at others with kindness and to act in a kind way toward others, realizing that this is what You expect each of us to do.

"Friends are attracted to kindness.
If I am kind, I will have kind friends."

Our previous Thought for the Day was about the need to treat others the way we want to be treated—primarily treating them with kindness.

Well, have you ever noticed that people who treat others with kindness have a lot more friends than those who treat others in an ugly way?

That's what it means when we say that friends are attracted to kindness. People want to be around those who are kind—primarily because they don't have to be afraid that those people are going to say something ugly to them. They can have fun with them and just be themselves with them.

Also, if they are kind to you, you will be kind to them as well. It just makes sense that if you are kind to others, you are going to have more friends and the more friends you have, the happier you will be.

Try it—you will be glad you did!

Dear God,

Help us to put into practice being kind to those around us. Help us to always treat others with kindness and to love and appreciate our friendships. Thank You for the blessing of friendship.

Day 10
Valentine's Day

"Valentine's Day is a day all about love. As God's children, we have the greatest love we could ever have—the love of our Father—our Lord and Savior, Jesus Christ."

God loves me! God loves each of you! We are so blessed! You know, for Valentine's Day, we often see hearts everywhere. Why is that? Well, you know, our physical heart is very important, isn't it? Our hearts beat all the time. We can't live without our physical heart.

For many years, because our hearts are so important, the shape of a heart has been used to symbolize love because of the importance of love in our lives. We automatically think "love" when we see a heart symbol.

However, love is from God. The Bible says God ***is*** love. That's hard to imagine—God actually ***being*** love.

Real love is given to us as a gift. We don't have to make any special promises, or do any special things for God to love us. He just does. God loves all of us, no matter what.

So today, as you think about Valentine's Day, remember the greatest love of all comes from above, and be blessed in that thought.

Dear God,

We thank You for the day we call Valentine's Day when we remember those we love and care about. Help us to remember, first and foremost, the love You have for us and help us to always place You first in all things.

Day 11

"Children, obey your parents in the Lord, for this is right. Honor your father and mother (this is the first commandment with promise), that it may go well with you and that you may live long in the land."

—Ephesians 6:1-3

Let's look at each of these verses and determine what they mean:

- "***Honor your father and mother***—What does that mean? It's more than just obeying. It is treating them with love and respect.
- ***This is the first commandment with promise***—What does that mean? It's the first of the Ten Commandments that comes with a specific promise from God; there is a reward if you do this right.
- ***That it may go well with you***—What does that mean? That God will help your life work out better, not perfect, but much better than it would be if you did not obey, love, and respect your parents.
- ***That you may live long in the land***—What does that mean? When God first said this, He was talking about the Promised Land, but for Christians, the Promised Land is Heaven" *(From Ministry-to-Children.com).*

So today, think of one way you can show your parents the respect they deserve. Remember how blessed you are to have the parents you have who love you so much.

Dear God,

Help us to remember how blessed we are to have people in our lives who love us the way they do. May we always be aware of the fact that we need to love and respect them more each day.

Day 12

"I will thank God for the gift He has given me."

God created you and me. He knows every little detail about us. He made each of us unique and there is no one created exactly like us in the whole world.

God has a purpose for each one of us. He has given us gifts or talents that we can use to help others see that God exists.

Many of us know clearly what our gifts or talents are and how God wants to use us in this life. Others may not yet know what their gift and purpose is in this life.

Someone once put it this way: "Our lives are like an unopened present. We have received a present, but we don't know exactly what is inside until we take the wrapping paper off the present.

As each of us walk with God, by faith, day by day, obeying His word, He begins to prepare us for what is inside that present. It may take a while, but He is getting us ready.

In God's perfect time, He allows the wrapping on the gift we have, to come off and He allows us to see what the talent or ability for serving Him will be.

You may not know what your gift or talent is right now, but God does and He already knows how you are going to use it for Him" (*Sermons4Kids*). Isn't that exciting?

Make sure you thank Him for that wonderful gift He has given you, whether you know what it is or not because, in His time, you will use it for Him if you remain faithful.

Dear God,

Thank you for each one of these precious students. In Your time, help each of them to see the talent You have given them, and help them to use it for Your glory!

Day 13

"I will respect others' things and their privacy."

What does the word privacy mean? It means something that is known only to a few people. It's kind of like a secret.

So our Thought for the Day means first, that we will respect others' things by not taking their things without asking permission. Second, we will respect their privacy by not sharing with others what they have told us that they don't want others to know.

How would you feel if someone went and got into your book bag without asking? You would probably be very upset, hurt, angry, or disappointed. However, what if they asked if they could borrow a pencil from your book bag? You would probably feel totally different, wouldn't you? All it would take is for someone to ask permission, not just go and take things without asking.

The same is true about things that you don't want others to know—private things. Maybe there is something that your friend told ***you only***—you respect their privacy by not telling others what they've said. It's the right thing to do.

So respect others by asking permission to borrow something they have or to look at something of theirs. In addition, respect them by keeping to yourself anything they have shared with you that is for you only.

God wants us to show respect always—whether it be to our parents, teachers, or our friends—respect is very important.

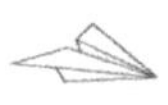

Dear God,

Help us to be respectful of others, whether it be asking permission to use something of theirs or keeping private what they have shared with us.

Day 14

"I am grateful for what I have and everyday I will say words of thanks for something I have."

When we think about all that so many in our world ***don't*** have, it makes us aware of all that we ***do*** have. There are so many in other countries who have so little. Many students in Kenya, who are your age, have so little, especially in their schools and villages. We are so blessed!

That's why it is so important for us to just take time each day to stop and thank the Lord for all He has given each of us. It would be a really good idea, as our Thought for the Day says, to thank God for one thing that you have each day. Each day it could be something different, but thank Him for it.

If you do this everyday, before too long, you will start to realize how many things you have to thank Him for. Then it won't take long to realize how fortunate you are and how He has showered you with His blessings.

So be grateful!! Thank God daily!! We are so blessed by the Lord!!

Dear God,

We thank You for everything that You have given each and everyone of us. Thank you for our families, our friends, our school, and our teachers. Thank You for daily supplying more than we need as we go through each and every day. We pray that we will never take these blessings for granted and that You will help us remember those who do not have much. Help us to reach out to them and be willing to share with them.

Day 15

"I have the courage to stand up for the Lord."

We have already talked about having courage to stand up for your friends when they are being mistreated, but this Thought for the Day is talking about having courage to stand up for the Lord. That's important as well.

When we are put in situations where others around us do not believe in the Lord as we do, we need to have the courage to stand up for Him. For instance, if someone starts questioning you as to why you believe in Jesus, you need to have the courage to say that you believe that Jesus is our Savior and that He died for our sins.

Courage, as we've talked about before, means standing up for what you know is right, without fear. Having courage is being brave, and speaking up for what you believe, even if others don't agree with you or criticize you.

It is wonderful to see someone stand up for the right thing. Being courageous isn't easy—it takes bravery. However, stop and think of the difference it can make. An entire activity can turn around, in a positive way, because someone took a stand. When someone knows they need to stand up in a circumstance and defend what they believe to be right, they are making an impression on others, even if they are unaware of it.

Knowing that we have stood up courageously should make all the difference in the world. The more we stand up for our faith, the firmer our faith becomes, and the happier we will be. Courage helps us press through our fears and do what we know is right.

Dear God,

Help us to have the attitude that we will stand up for You no matter what.

Day 16

"I will always tell the truth, no matter what."

Our Thought for the Day is very simple, isn't it? Just tell the truth. You know, telling the truth is part of being honest. When we tell the truth, we tell about things exactly as they happened.

Jesus always told the truth. You know, before Jesus was crucified (or killed), the soldiers took Him and they asked Him many questions. One of the questions they asked was, "Art Thou the Christ?"

Now Jesus knew that if He said He was the Christ, they would not let Him go and He would be killed, but He said, "I am." He told the truth.

He always told the truth, even when it was hard to do so and that's what we need to do, too. We need to be truthful, even when it is hard. Jesus always told the truth and He wants us to always tell the truth.

Always choose to do what is right. When you tell the truth, you are choosing the right thing.

Dear God,

Help us to choose to do the right things and to always be honest and tell the truth, no matter what. Help us to be good examples of what You want us to be.

Day 17

"God can work through suffering to accomplish His purposes in our lives."

You know, none of us like to go through difficult things. It's no fun, but what we must remember is that God is in control.

He allows the good and the bad things in life and we can trust Him to work all things together for good in the lives of those who love Him (Romans 8:28). That's important to remember.

There are so many people who have spent their whole lives working for the Lord and His purpose. Through doing this, they have touched so many and have impacted countless lives. And yet, some of them experience illnesses or they go through difficult things.

An example of this very thing is in the story of a Youth Pastor named Len. Len had worked his whole adult life with the youth of his church, influencing them in the way of the Lord. Len was diagnosed with cancer, but rather than dwell on himself, he got online and daily posted inspirational/uplifting comments to encourage and help others.

So many were impacted by his positive attitude, even during a difficult time. He chose to lift up the Lord, even during his struggles. Pastor Len has gone to be with the Lord now, but the impact he had on others, even during his own struggles, should never be underestimated.

God uses struggles to speak to others. God weaves the fabric in our lives. We will have happy and sad times, but God is an expert at bringing good out of bad. That's what we must all remember.

Dear God,

Help us to remember that You are in control of all things and that, even through difficult circumstances, You can turn that around for good. You can do all things.

Day 18

"Jesus is the best example of what God wants us to be."

Now, let's bring this down to where you all are right now. Have you ever thought about what Jesus was like when He was a child, maybe around your age?

Luke 2:41-52 gives us the following facts about Jesus as a young boy:

- "Jesus was truly a young boy. He was both human and fully God. He was very similar to each of you.
- He was a young boy who grew daily, and who learned things, just like you do.
- Jesus had Bible teachers all around Him and He listened carefully to each of them.

- Jesus obeyed His parents.
- Jesus was a young boy and He experienced many things that were very difficult for Him. However, He always did the right thing and gave us a good example to follow" *(Sundayschoolsources.com)*.

Jesus is the best example we have of what we need to be like—follow His example and you can't go wrong.

Dear God

You are the best example any of us have as to how to live our lives. Thank You for being our good example and help us all to strive to live by Your example.

Day 19

"I believe in myself. God made me unique and special. I will remember how special God thinks I am and I will feel good about myself."

Although we know that God made us in a very special way, sometimes we don't always see how unique and special we are. We sometimes get down on ourselves and we don't appreciate ourselves the way God wants us to.

Someone recently published the following to give you seven ways to appreciate yourself:

1. "Be careful about comparing yourself to other people. Sometimes that can make you feel good or even inspire you to improve in some way. However, sometimes it can make you overlook what's truly good about yourself and cause you to feel bad.
2. Think about times when you've done something good. Include those times when you've made a difference for somebody else by being helpful, kind, or thoughtful.
3. Take part in activities that make you feel good such as reading, sports, or spending time with good friends.
4. Don't be so afraid of "messing up" that you're not willing to try something new.
5. New experiences can help you grow and discover wonderful new things about yourself.
6. When you do mess up at something, don't get down on yourself. Think about what you can learn from the experience and how you can do better next time.
7. Think about the things you do well.

Remember, the most important thing is what we're like inside—not what we own or what we've accomplished" *(kidsofintegrity.com).*

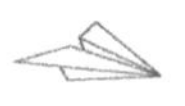

Dear God,

Thank you for making each of us in Your own very unique way. Help us to remember the special things that You have instilled within each of us.

Day 20

"When I am sad, I help myself feel better by thinking about all of the good things that God has given me."

You know, all of us feel sad sometime. That's just the way it is in life. But one thing that always helps us feel better is to think about all the things that God has blessed us with.

Chances are, that if you stop to think about all the good things in your life right now, they would far outnumber the bad things. We have so many wonderful blessings!

So when you start to feel sad, turn it around and look at the good things in your life. You will not be sad for long if you do.

Listen to this poem by a man named Ogden Nash:

Now another day is breaking, Sleep was sweet and so is waking.
Dear Lord, I promised you last night, Never again to sulk or fight.
Such vows are easier to keep, When a child is sound asleep. Today,
O Lord, for your dear sake, I'll try to keep them when awake.

So be happy today. God has blessed each of us mightily and we have nothing to be sad about.

Dear God,

When we start to feel unhappy, redirect our thoughts, and let us remember how much we have.

Day 21

"I like those who are different from me. I can learn a lot from them. They are my friends."

All of us are made in the image of God and we are all special. We are all the body of Christ and we are called to work together and accomplish the work of the church.

Someone once wrote: "We all have eyes, but they all look different. We all have hair, but we all have different color hair. We all wear clothes and shoes, but we wear all different types. We all have families, but we have different people in our families. We are all different ages, we all have different favorite colors, and so on. We are all unique! God also made us different in the way we think and act. We all have different likes and act in different ways" *(kidsofintegrity).*

Just because we are different, doesn't mean we can't get along. Each one of us brings something unique to our friendships. We can each learn from one another. That's how God intended it to be. Friends—unique and different—Learning from one another.

Dear God,

Thank You for our uniqueness. Thank You for creating us and shaping us into the people You want us to be. Help us to recognize Your plan for our lives and to strive to do all we can to fulfill that plan.

MARCH

Day 1

"Jesus knows us. He is our good shepherd and we are His sheep."

You know, Jesus is like a good shepherd who knows and loves his sheep, and guess what? ***We*** are His sheep.

Someone once published several facts about sheep and their shepherds:

1. "Sheep will only respond to, and go to, their shepherd.
2. A good shepherd will lay down his life to save his sheep.
3. Jesus describes Himself as The Good Shepherd.
4. The sheep recognize their own shepherd by his voice.
5. Jesus says He knows His sheep like the Father knows Him, and
6. Jesus died for His sheep"—that's us *(kidssundayschool.com)*.

When we think about Jesus being the Good Shepherd to us who are His sheep, it helps us realize that Jesus wants to have a relationship with those He loves. What a blessing!

Since we have a relationship with Jesus, He talks to us through His word, and through the Holy Spirit. He tells us to love one another, be kind, obey our parents, be good examples, and many other things.

Jesus is the Good Shepherd and we are His sheep. Aren't we glad we have a Shepherd who loves and cares for us so much?

Dear God,

Thank You for being our Good Shepherd and for loving us so much. Help us to truly appreciate the relationship we have with You and to listen as You guide us daily.

Day 2

"Students with good habits are more successful."

First, what is success? Success means accomplishing what you set out to do. Now, what is a habit? A habit is something we do over and over.

So "students with good habits are more successful…" means that students who have a good routine or schedule are able to accomplish what they set out to do. Now how do you do that?

We have heard it said that it only takes 21 days, or three weeks, for something you do to become a habit. That means either a good habit, or a bad one. For example, let's say that you want to start to do things that will help you make better grades. Let's say that you go home everyday and you immediately start doing your homework. If you continue to do the same thing everyday for at least three weeks, then it will become a good habit and you will continue to do that because then it will become a natural thing for you. This, in turn, will help you in your studies, making you more successful with your grades.

In the same way, if you continue to do something negative over a period of time, it will be easy for you to continue in this negative behavior. This, in turn, will keep you from success.

One of the most important things you can do is develop good habits and break bad ones. Bad habits form more easily because they don't take as much effort. It's the easy way out.

So today, start thinking about what bad habits you can break and what good habits you can start. God can help you break those bad ones and start those good ones.

Dear God,

Help us, Lord, to create good habits and break bad ones so we can become all that You have meant us to be.

Day 3

"God expects us to be responsible."

What does it mean to be responsible? If you look up the meaning of "responsible", you will find the following: It means, "Taking care of the things we are suppose to do." It means, "Answering for what we have, or have not, done." It means, "Making good decisions."

God expects that we do all those things to the best of our ability. He expects us to be responsible.

There is a choice we all have to make in everything we do and we must remember that the choice we make is very important to God. We want to do the right thing and be responsible.

What can we do to be responsible? Someone once came up with the following list of items we can do to be responsible. Listen and try to always do these things to show responsibility:

1. "Take responsibility for your actions. Don't make excuses or blame others.
2. Always do your best.
3. Admit your mistakes and learn from them.
4. Be sure and do what you say you will do.
5. Don't keep others waiting; be on time.
6. Always keep your promises, in word or deed" *(Character Trait Poster).*

Follow these guidelines and you will have a great start at being responsible. You will make God very happy.

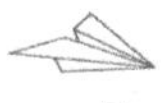

Dear God,

Help us to be responsible people; people You are proud of. Help us to do the things that You would have us do always.

Day 4

"Jesus loves us so much and we can follow His example by loving others too."

God commands us to love Him and to love one another as He has loved us. You know, God showed us His great love for us by dying for our sins on the cross.

Therefore, it is only right that He would expect us to love others and follow His example. We need to stop and think about ways we can show love to particular people throughout the week and then do it!

As we've said, love is a command from God. Jesus says, "Love the Lord your God with all your heart, and with all your soul, and with all your mind." God is love, and God showed His love for us by sending Jesus to die for us.

We need to follow that example and show love to one another by putting others first and thinking of them more than ourselves. We need to love them.

"It has been said that after we truly believe that love is from God, His love for us, and our love for Him, can overflow into the people around us. It will be a very natural thing" *Sermons4kids).*

Your love for them will be an obvious thing, and you might find that by loving them, they will easily begin to love you back. That is usually the way it works!

Dear God,

Help us to remember throughout our day, how much You love us and want us to love others. Help us to look for opportunities to love others by helping them, talking with them, and just being a friend to them when they need someone.

Day 5

"A friendship grows when you plant a seed of kindness."

Have you ever thought about that? Think about the friends you have. Being friends with those people didn't just happen. You are friends for a reason. You became friends because you saw something in them you liked, and they saw something in you they liked.

Just like a garden where seeds are sown and beautiful things grow, if you plant a seed of kindness in another person's heart, their feelings for you will grow. Over time, you will have a special friendship.

Someone once put it this way: "Seeds of kindness attach themselves to another by creating feelings of affection. That seed of kindness grows friends who help each other, who share their feelings with each other, and who share joys and sorrows with each other" *(kidsofintegrity.com).*

When you plant a seed of kindness, friendship grows into something to be treasured forever.

Listen to this poem:

Friends smile at you, They like your face. They want to be with you, Any old place. Friends have fun with you. Friends share. They're glad when you're happy, When you're sad, they care. If you're a friend, Then you care, too. That's why your friends Are glad you're YOU! (Tooter4Kids)

Dear God,

Thank you for our beautiful friendships. Help us to never take them for granted and to work hard to be the good friend to others that we need to be.

Day 6

"Jesus knows and cares about us when we are sad."

Do you ever get sad? We all get sad sometime, don't we? Well, God knows when we are sad. Sometimes you will have days that are just not good ones. Sad things happen to everyone, but the Bible says that God knows all about our sorrows, or the sad things in our lives.

Jesus is the one to help us during our times of sorrow. Someone once put it this way:

1. ***"Jesus is our Doctor***. He knows what we need to feel better. Stay close to Him and pray for His help.
2. ***Jesus is our Master Potter***. A potter is a kind of artist that makes beautiful things from clay. The Bible says that we are like a piece of clay in the hands of God. Even though difficult things happen to all of us, God molds and shapes those difficulties in our lives so that something good comes from them.
3. ***Jesus is the head***. Your head is at the top of your body. It's where you do all of your thinking. Jesus should be the head of our bodies. Let Him give you the thoughts that you should have. Thoughts of joy to comfort your sadness" *(SelfGrowth.com)*.

He knows and understands everything. He knows you better than you know yourself. He is The One who can make you feel better.

Dear God,

Help us remember that when we feel sad, we can always ask You to help us because You know us better than we know ourselves. You will always be there for us to comfort us.

Day 7

"I will have the courage to stand up for my friends who are being teased or picked on by others."

We have addressed several times standing up for the right thing. This is a very important thing because God expects us to stand up and say no to those things that are wrong.

So, if we see someone who is being teased or picked on, we need to find the courage to stand up for them. In addition, we need to make sure that those who are doing the teasing know that this is not what God wants us to do.

If we do this, we will be showing the person who is being picked on that they have someone who cares enough to speak up for them. In addition, we will also speak to those who are doing what they shouldn't be doing in a form of correction.

It takes courage to do this, but God will honor this if we follow through with it. It is the right thing to do, and God will bless us if we do the right thing.

Dear God,

Please give us all courage to do the right thing, even when it is very difficult. Remind us that You are with us every minute and that with You by our side, we can do anything.

Day 8

"I will strive to be a good sport by following the rules, taking turns, and playing fair."

You know, all of us like to play games, don't we? It's fun. When you go out to play on the playground or when you are playing a game in gym class, it's a fun time.

However, when someone is not playing fair or following the rules of the game, it takes the fun away from everyone. God is not pleased when we don't take turns, follow the rules, or play fair.

He wants us to always do the right thing. Your game time can be so much more fun if you play the game the way God wants you to play the game. Even if you are not the winner of the game, give kind words to the person who is. Be a good sport. We have often heard the phrase, "It is not all about winning or losing, it's how you play the game." How true that is. The way you handle yourself when playing sports, says a lot more about you than winning does.

So today, be a good sport when you are playing and help everyone have a fun time. God will be pleased by this.

Dear God,

Help us to remember to be good sports, whether we are playing on the playground, playing a game in gym class, or even playing in the classroom. Help us remember to take turns and play fair so that all of us can have fun.

Day 9

"Jesus wants me to obey Him."

We often talk about having joy in our hearts. The Lord has done so much for us that this brings joy to our heart. However, we need to bring joy to the Lord's heart in return.

One very important way to bring joy to the Lord's heart is by obeying Him. Let's think about how we can obey the Lord Jesus and do what He wants us to do.

In His word, the Lord tells us things that we should not do. The Bible says, "You shall not steal" (Exodus 20:15). We all know that we should not take things that don't belong to us. However, sometimes it may be easy to think, "No one will see me." But the Lord sees and knows all things. When we take things that are not ours, we are disobeying the Lord.

Also, the Bible says, "Lie not one to another…" (Colossians 3:9). This is a command that we all can understand. God hates lying lips! If we don't tell the truth, we are not obeying the Lord.

The Lord not only tells us the things that we should not do, but He also tells us things that we should do. The Bible says that we should be kind and forgiving people, following God's example in all things.

When you are in doubt about doing something, ask yourself this question: "Would Jesus want me to do this?" If you think that He does not want you to do it, don't do it! If it is right for you to do it, the Lord will help you to know it is the right thing to do.

We obey the Lord in the way that pleases Him when we do what we are told to do, when we are told to do it, with a good attitude. It's that simple! That makes Him very happy.

Dear Lord,

Thank You for your goodness and mercy. Thank You for loving us, even when we mess up.

Day 10

"When I listen, I show others that I care about them."

Did you know that? When you take the time to stop and listen to others, you are showing them respect, and you are showing them that you care about them enough to listen to what they have to say.

Have you ever tried to talk to a friend and they are so busy talking, and not listening, that they don't hear a thing you say? That's very frustrating, isn't it? You end up feeling like they really don't care about what you are saying or even care about you.

When we stop and listen to others, we are showing them respect. We are saying that we care enough about them that we want to hear what they have to say.

So today, try extra hard to stop and listen, because when you do that, you are showing that you care about others. It's the right thing to do.

Dear God,

Help us to be good listeners today and to stop and give others the respect they deserve by hearing what they have to say.

Day 11

"I will think for myself, make smart choices, and do what God would have me do, not what my friends want me to do."

Do you ever find yourself getting caught up in doing what all your classmates want you to do, even if it isn't the right thing? It's very tempting to listen to our friends and do what they want, isn't it?

Sometimes we give in to our friends, don't we? That's when it is important to remember that the only one you need to please is the Lord. Always ask yourself if it is something that the Lord would approve of.

That's what it means to think for yourself because even if everyone else is doing it, that doesn't make it right. You need to think for yourself. You do not need to be persuaded by your friends to do something the Lord would not approve of.

So today, be your own person. Be God's disciple, and do what is right, not what others want you to do. Do what God wants you to do.

Dear God,

We pray that you will give us wisdom, respect, and guidance to always strive to be the people You want us to be. Help us to think for ourselves, and do only those things that You would approve of.

Day 12

"I need to try to understand what my friends are feeling."

Have you ever had one of your friends come to school rather sad? Chances are that you didn't know why, and you really didn't know what to say. Right? We all have.

Well, when this happens, you can show yourself to be a true friend to them by trying to understand their feelings. Try to think about how you feel sometimes when you are sad, and just give them a kind word. Help them refocus on the good things they have.

You have the opportunity during those times to help your friends feel better by just trying to be understanding. Maybe all they need is a kind word from you.

You have the opportunity to help someone a great deal. By just trying to understand how they feel and by using your understanding to help them feel better, you are making a difference in their lives. By doing this, you are doing what God would have you do. That makes everything better.

Dear God,

Help us to do what You would have us do to assist others, especially our friends, when they are having a bad day or when they are just sad. Help us try to understand how they are feeling and to give them a kind word to help them refocus on the good things in their lives.

Day 13

"Everyone makes mistakes sometimes so when I make a mistake, I will not get angry with myself or others, but instead, I will try to do better."

If someone asked you the question, "Have you ever made a mistake?" what would you answer? Obviously, you would say, "Yes", because we all make mistakes. There is no one who doesn't make mistakes. We are human and we mess up.

Obviously, we don't mean to make mistakes, but they happen, don't they? How we respond when we make a mistake is the important thing.

First of all, we need to admit that we have made a mistake. We need to always be willing to accept the fact that when we do something we shouldn't have, we say we did something wrong. It says a lot about a person when they are willing to admit their wrongs.

Next, we need to pray to the Lord and ask for forgiveness. If we have wronged someone else, we need to ask for their forgiveness too.

Like our Thought for the Day says, we don't need to get mad at ourselves or others, but instead, try hard to do better. We learn from our mistakes.

We are not perfect people. We wouldn't be here on this earth if we were perfect; only God is perfect. We are going to make mistakes, but we need to respond appropriately when we do and try to do better. Learn from your mistakes and try not to make those same mistakes again.

Dear God,

Thank You that You love us in spite of the many mistakes that we so often make. Help us to respond the way You would have us respond when we do something that You would not have us do. Help us to admit our mistakes, be repentant of them, and help us to do better the next time.

Day 14

"We need to treat everyone with respect."

The word, respect, means to honor or have a high opinion of. So our Thought for the Day truly means that we need to respect everyone we meet by honoring them and showing them that we have a high opinion of them.

Students, in the classroom, you need to show respect for your teachers. You do this by doing what they say to do without grumbling, complaining, giving them bad looks, or simply not doing what they say to do.

In the Bible, Hebrews 13:17 says to obey your leaders and submit to them. Submit means to accept what they say to do.

However, respect goes even further than respecting your teacher. It means respecting each person that you come in contact with—your classmates, your parents, your bus driver, the mailman, and we could go on and on. It means to show respect to everyone you come in contact with.

So think about respect today. Treat everyone with respect and God will have a smile on His face when He looks at you today. Do the right thing and make it a wonderful day!

Dear God,

Help us to respect everyone that we come in contact with today. Help us to honor all those around us and to strive to be the respectful people that You want us to be.

Day 15

"I work out my problems without hurting others."

Have you ever just had a bad day and you end up taking it out on someone else? Maybe you are grumpy with your parents, or you say something unkind to one of your classmates? We have all done that, haven't we?

We all have bad days sometimes. Most of the time, when we do have a bad day, we end up lashing out at other people, don't we?

Let's remember that we should always work out whatever is bothering us without hurting others in the process. You can never take back the words you speak. Make sure they are not unkind words spoken in a moment of anger because you are not having a good day. God isn't happy with that, and this should not be acceptable to us either.

Remember, there is a better way to work out your problems without hurting other people—it's called prayer. Stop and pray and ask God to help you through it all, and chances are, that you will feel much better and no one will be hurt in the process.

Dear God,

We thank You for this day and for all that You have given us. Help us to focus on You when we have a tendency to get upset and say things we don't need to say.

Day 16

"I am being polite when I wait for my turn,
be a good sport, and say please and thank you."

We all know that having manners is very important. We know how much it means to others when we say thank you when they have done something for us, and how respectful it is when we say please, as well. Most of us do this everyday with no problem.

However, waiting our turn, or being a good sport, might be a bit more difficult for some of us. You know, though, that this is just as important as saying thank you and please.

It is a bit more difficult because we all want to get in there and play the game so we don't want to wait to play. We want to play right away. We also want to win at those games because, most of us, have a competitive nature and ***we*** want to win! However, there is a right and a wrong way to approach each of these things.

When you are out on the playground or in your gym class, just wait your turn and be happy if someone else wins at a game. You will have a chance the next time. If you just do the right thing, you will enjoy the game much more.

So, be polite in every situation, and you will find that you will have a much better day. It's what God wants you to do!

Dear God,

Help us to make You proud today by doing the right thing in every situation. Help us remember to be polite always, and to show others that we respect them by the way we treat them, and by the way we talk to them.

Day 17

"I need to encourage my friends to do their best."

Do you know what it means to encourage others? It means that you say things that will give others courage to do something they need to do, or you support them in some way. You say things that will build them up.

Obviously, you already know that ***you*** need to do your best always, but it can mean a lot if you encourage or say things to your friends that will cause them to do their best as well. You know, the Lord always wants us to do everything, as unto Him.

We need to do everything we are doing as if we are doing it for the Lord. That makes a big difference when you start to think about it like that, doesn't it?

Sometimes just encouraging your friends to do their best on their class work, or on their homework, or even encouraging them to read more can really make a difference. Sometimes we will listen to our friends before we will listen to anyone else. You could make a big difference.

Be an encourager today. Encourage your friends to do what you already know that you need to do as well, and that is, to do their best. If it comes from you, their friend, that can make a big difference to them. Try it and see.

Dear God,

Help us to always do our best in everything, and to remember that when we do, we are doing this, as unto You. Help us encourage our friends and others to always do their best as well. May we be known as encouragers.

Day 18

"The Lord will always guide me to do what is right."

Isn't that a wonderful thought? If we allow the Lord to be the center of our lives, and if we have Him deep in our heart, He will guide us in the way that we should go.

You know, if we were to try to guide ourselves daily, without the Lord in control, we would probably get into a lot of trouble. When we start relying on ourselves and leave God out of things, then that is when we start seeing that we have more problems than good things.

So today, stop and think: "Am I allowing the Lord to guide me today?" If you are not, you need to turn things around quickly because you will have a much better day if you allow yourself to be guided by the Lord. In the end, He is going to guide you to do what is right.

Dear God,

We thank You for being our God and for guiding us in the right way. Help us to allow You to do Your marvelous work in us today and to guide us in the way we should go.

Day 19

"I will live each day with honesty."

If someone asked you what it means to be honest, most of you could answer that question without any hesitation. It means to be truthful, not just in what you say, but in what you do.

You know, all of us have many opportunities everyday to tell the truth, don't we? And for the most part, that is not that hard for us to do because we know how God feels about that.

However, sometimes, it's a little more difficult for us to be honest in what we do. Now what does that mean? Someone once wrote the following list to help us get a true meaning of honesty:

- "Honesty is not to make promises that we are not planning to keep.
- Honesty is following the rules.
- Honesty is doing our own work and not copying someone else's.
- Honesty is returning things that others let us use.
- Honesty is accepting our mistakes and correcting them.
- Honesty is not taking things that don't belong to us" *(Kids of Integrity).*

This is a good list to help us check ourselves and make sure that we are being honest always, not just in what we say, but in what we do. Live each day with honesty. You will be happier, others around you will be happier, and you will make God very happy with you.

Dear God,

Help us to do those things that are honest and pure. Help us to be helpful, honest, and respectful. May we give You all the glory for any good that we do.

Day 20

"When I am angry, I will use self-control and act the way God wants me to act."

We all get angry sometimes, don't we? But it really says a lot about us, if when we get angry, we use our self-control and act the way God wants us to act.

Do you know what self-control is? It is when you stop yourself from doing things you want to do, but which may not be good for you to do.

For instance, maybe a classmate takes something away from you. You may want to hit the person or say something really ugly to them. However, if you use your self-control, instead of hitting them or speaking unkind words to them, you raise your hand quietly and let your teacher know what happened so that she can handle it.

That's self-control. It is keeping yourself from getting caught up in something that could get you in trouble. It is thinking before you act.

So today, remember, if things don't go the way you want them to go and you get angry, use your self-control. Act the way God would want you to act.

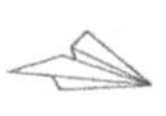

Dear God,

Help us to use our self-control today when things don't go the way we want them to go. Help us to keep a good attitude and to do the things You would have us do.

Day 21

"I am being creative when I play music, draw, paint, write a poem or a story. God can be glorified when I use my creative gifts to praise Him."

What does creative mean? It means that we come up with new ideas and we use our imagination to create new ways of doing normal things. That is clever, don't you think?

God has gifted all of us in one way or another. Some of you are very talented musically, some of you are great artists, some are great writers, but all of you have been gifted somehow.

When you use your creative gifts (such as playing music, drawing a picture, writing, and so forth), you can use those to give God the praise for gifting you with them. We have seen students who, as they get older, use their musical talents in worship services where they praise the Lord; and we've heard of students who have had articles published in books (those articles spoke about their faith in the Lord).

So if God cared enough to bless you with a creative talent, remember that you can give back to Him by using that talent to honor Him. We all look forward to seeing what you are going to do for Him in the future.

Dear God,

As we go through this day, help us remember to do the things You would have us do. Remind us, as we are using the gifts You have blessed us with, to always use them to honor You.

Day 22

"When I use my time wisely, there is usually enough time to do what I want to do."

Have you ever really thought about that? If you sit down and do your homework and stay focused until you are finished, chances are, that you will get done much sooner. That means, that you will then have more time to do what you really want to do.

In one class recently, the students were all working quietly on their work and everyone got finished. The teacher announced that because they had all attended to their work so well, that they were going to have time to do an art project. The students were thrilled because that was what they really preferred to do.

So think about it—if you don't waste your time, don't look around, but rather work diligently on what you need to be doing, you will get done much sooner. If that's the case, you will come up with something really fun to do with all the extra time you have.

Try it! Chances are that you will be pleasantly surprised with all the extra time you will have to do fun things.

Dear God,

Help us to use our time wisely and to stay focused on the tasks at hand. When we start to get distracted from doing what we need to be doing, please refocus us.

Day 23

"I look for what is good in others and I say what I like about them."

You know, that's important, isn't it? Have you ever had someone come up to you and say, "Do you know what I like about you? You are always..." And then they finish the sentence by saying what they like about you. Have you ever had that happen?

It probably doesn't happen as much as we would like for it to happen. Why is that? Well, sometimes, we just don't think about the good things in others; sometimes, we are too quick to look at the bad or the things we ***don't*** like.

That's sad, isn't it? Everyone has been created by God and they are very special. Everyone has good things about them. What we need to do is look for the good things and point them out to them. Do you know that if you did that once each day, you could really make others feel wonderful? You would make their day!!

Why don't you try that today? Pick one person and tell them what you like about them. You will put a smile on their face!

Listen to this poem:

Little deeds of kindness, Little words of love, Help to make earth happy, Like the heaven above (Julia Fletcher Carney).

Dear God,

Help us to be people who look for the good in others. Help us to focus on what we like about others, not what bothers us. Help us to put away a judgmental spirit and to be positive.

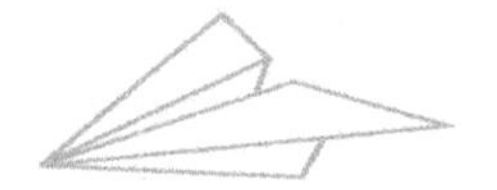

APRIL

Day 1

"I appreciate my family for all they have done, and still do, for me."

What is a family? I bet the first answer you come up with is your mom, dad, sisters, and brothers, but God provided us with more family than just our parents, brothers, and sisters. He has given us our uncles, aunts, cousins, and grandparents as well. He has purposely surrounded us with this great group of people to help us through life.

And, you know what? God loves everyone in our family and He works to make sure that they help us when we need it. Giving us a family is part of His plan for us.

God gives us families to support us, guide us in our choices we make, and help us in times of trouble. That's wonderful, isn't it?

You know, God has given us the freedom to make our own choices, but He has given us family members to help us and guide us as we make those choices. They help us in all that we do. Aren't you glad you have a family?

We can talk to them and get their guidance always. They are our support when we need help. We should always show them how much we love and appreciate them because they do so much for us.

Dear God,

Thank you for being our God and for loving us so much that You would give us very special people in our lives called a family. Help us to never take them for granted and to always let them know how much we love and appreciate them.

Day 2

"Smiling is contagious. I smile at everyone. I smile at the bus driver, at my teachers, my friends, and all the people that I meet. When I smile, others usually smile back."

Have you ever noticed that? When we smile at others, most of the time, they can't help but smile back. Sometimes people may have a really mean look on their face, but when we smile at them, their whole expression changes.

Sometimes people have a lot of things going on and they may not necessarily feel like smiling, but when someone gives them a smile, they really can't do anything else but smile back. This warms their heart to see someone treating them kindly. So try smiling at others and see what a good response you get.

This poem says it all—it's called *Smiling*:

Smiling is contagious; you catch it like the flu. When someone smiled at me today, I started smiling too. I passed around a corner and someone saw my grin. When he smiled, I realized I had passed it on to him. I thought about that smile and then I realized its worth. A single smile, just like mine, could travel around the earth. So if you feel a smile begin, don't leave it undetected. Let's start an epidemic quick, and get the world infected. (altern8ives)

Try smiling all day. I bet you'll be surprised at how much more pleasant your day will be.

Dear God,

Help us to be the friend to others that we need to be. Lord, help us smile today.

Day 3

"I cannot predict the future, but I know who holds my future in His hands."

Most of you have probably given some thought to what you'd like to do when you grow up. It's truly exciting to think about what job you may have in the future, or where you may end up living.

Some of you may find yourself thinking, “I’d like to be a doctor, or I’d like to be a teacher, or I’d like to be…” well, you fill in the blank. There are so many things you could do and it is so exciting to think about what you may choose to do.

Whether you end up doing what you think you’d like to do remains to be seen, but one thing is for sure. God has a plan for you and He is going to map your life out in such a way that He is going to put you exactly where He wants you.

God has a plan for each of His children and we just have to trust that He will put us where He wants us to be in the future. We must listen to Him and follow His direction.

Remember, you don’t know what your future holds, but you know who holds your future and that should make you feel very happy. We are looking forward to seeing the plans that God has for each of you.

Dear God,

Thank you for all the plans You have for each one of us. Lord, we pray that we will be obedient to Your will for our lives and let You take control. Use us as You want to use us.

Day 4

“I take care of myself by sleeping and resting enough. I understand that my body needs the rest to rejuvenate, to restore its energy and to be in focus.”

You know, one of the biggest things you can do to make sure you will be able to do your best on your school work is to get enough rest so that you will be alert and focused. Rest is essential to our well-being.

Did you know that getting enough rest and sleep helps keep you healthy? When you sleep at night, your brain is resting too, and getting you ready for the next day.

When sleeping, your muscles get stronger, and different parts of your body are once again put in order to get you ready for a brand new day. It is very similar to recharging a car, except that you are recharging your body.

Getting enough rest is necessary for your body to be healthy, and it determines whether you feel good or bad the next day. If you've gotten enough rest at night you will feel, think, and perform your best.

So, when your mom and dad say, "It's time to go to bed", listen and remember that getting the rest you need will make you happier the next day. Mom and Dad always know best!!

Dear God,

Thank you for a brand new day. Lord, You have made our bodies to function perfectly. We have been created in a very special way by You. Thank You for that. Help us to do our part to take care of our bodies. Help us to get the rest we need so that we can be healthy, alert, and the best we can be.

Day 5

"Think right, do right, feel right."

Do you know what determines the kind of person you will be? It is not your looks, or how smart you are, or how much money you have. It is what you think and believe.

What you think determines what you do and what you feel. When we think right thoughts, we do right things, and we have right feelings. However, when we think wrong thoughts, we do wrong things, and we have wrong or unpleasant feelings.

Wrong thoughts come from the Devil. The Devil puts wrong thoughts into the minds of people and these wrong thoughts lead to wrong actions and wrong feelings.

The Devil makes us think that the things that make a person worth something are good looks, being smart, and having a lot of money. This is a lie that the Devil puts in our heads.

God loves and respects a poor person as much as He does a rich person. He loves and respects a child as much as He loves and respects a grown-up.

God says in His word that He loves and respects all of us. We are very precious to Him. We will always be His children. He does not love one over another.

This is what is meant by right thoughts. Right thoughts lead to right actions and right feelings.

Begin thinking right thoughts now. Keep saying to yourself, "God loves me. God respects me. I am very precious to Him. I want to be His child forever." Thinking these right thoughts will help you do the right things, and you will feel better about yourself. Try it!

Dear God,

Help us focus on good thoughts, not negative ones, and to remember how much You love and respect each one of us. Help us choose good thoughts daily to encourage those around us.

Day 6

"Courage doesn't always roar: sometimes courage is the quiet voice at the end of the day saying, 'I will try again tomorrow.'"

What is courage? Courage means being brave. It is facing and dealing with anything seen as dangerous, difficult, or painful instead of running from it.

It has been said that you don't always have to be loud and roar like a lion to be brave. Sometimes the bravest people are those who face their fears and try again to overcome them.

A courageous person is a person who admits that he did something wrong and is ready to accept the consequences of his behavior. A courageous person is one who is willing to do what is right even though it is hard. A courageous person is one who makes tough decisions and follows through on those decisions.

Think of one thing you are afraid of. Think of ways you can overcome that fear. It may be a fear of speaking in front of a group of people or a fear of climbing. Maybe it is a fear of standing up for the right things when others are doing wrong. We all have fears. What is important is how we respond to our fears.

Work to overcome your fears. Try and try again. That's courage!

Dear God,

Help us to be courageous and to face our fears by trying daily to overcome those things we are fearful of. Help us to show courage by not giving up when things are hard for us, but by trying again.

Day 7

"I treat everyone with respect."

First of all, what is respect? We've talked about this before, but respect is treating people and things with kindness and care. Within our school, you are expected to respect both your teacher and those in charge, as well as your classmates.

What exactly does that mean? That means that if your teacher asks you to do something, you say, "Yes, ma'am" and you do it without asking why. If your teacher asks everyone to look at her while she is talking, you look at her—no question about it. You do what she says every time she asks something of you.

How do you show respect to your classmates? If they are talking, you listen to them without interrupting. You share with them, help them, and be kind to them. This is respecting them.

There are many ways you can show respect, but the most important thing is that ***you do show respect always***. This is what we call "a life lesson" because this is something you will need to do throughout your lifetime in your future jobs, in college, or wherever you go. Learn respect for others—it's what God expects us to do.

Dear God,

Teach us respect and what it means in the environment around us. Thank you for these students who are such good examples in this area. They are truly a blessing to all, by the respect they show others. Lord, keep growing that in them and make it a part of who they are.

Day 8

"When I work and when I'm helpful to others, I feel good."

Being productive and helpful is a wonderful blessing that God has given us. Don't you feel good when you have worked hard, have completed a job, and have been successful in it? God created all of us to feel satisfied when we work and are successful.

When we work, we get things done. God planned this for us. It is a part of His purpose for us here on earth. In addition, when we work to help other people that makes our purpose even bigger. When we help others, we feel good about what we are doing to benefit those around us.

God has a purpose for everything He has created. Someone once wrote the following about the purpose of even the animals that God created: "Animals and insects were created with a purpose. The Lord designed them in such a way that they naturally work and build things for themselves and their families. Squirrels store up their food to last all through the winter until spring comes around again. The ant is another example of not being lazy. Even though the ant doesn't have a 'boss', it still works very hard" *(umcmission.org).* Just like these animals, God created us to be hard workers with a purpose.

When we help others, we are "paying forward" the blessings that God has given us. When we do this, we will feel good about ourselves because we will know that this is what God wants us to do. God will reward us in His time. What a wonderful thought!

Dear God,

Thank you for the abilities you have given each of us to work and to be helpful to those around us. Help us to remember that this is what You want each of us to do on a daily basis.

Day 9

"When I have a problem, I will work on a way to solve it, without hurting others."

All of you can think of a time when you had, what you thought, was a big problem. Maybe you asked your parents if you could go play at your friend's house, but you hadn't done your homework so they said no. Maybe you and your brother or sister got in trouble with your parents for doing something you shouldn't have done.

Those are problems, aren't they? They are problems because you don't feel good about the way things have worked out, and probably, you feel badly because you know that what you did wasn't right.

Well, the first thing you should do is ask the Lord to help you come up with how you should solve the problem. Always pray to the Lord and ask Him to guide you in solving the problem.

If you ask for His help, He is going to give you the right thing to do. Sometimes we try to solve our problems on our own and when we do, we end up hurting others in the process. For instance, what if, when you and your brother or sister got in trouble with your parents, you tried to get yourself out of it by blaming your sibling. That's when your actions hurt others.

You can't do that because it is the wrong thing to do. Use the right method to solve your problem. The Lord may have you simply apologize to your parents and accept the consequences of your actions. If so, that's what's best.

Trust God to guide you in your problem-solving issues. He is the best Guide you have.

Dear God,

When we are faced with problems, help us to seek Your guidance in coming to a solution that is in Your will.

Day 10

"I do not take what is not mine."

You know, God has blessed us with so much, and He wants us to be happy with what we have. If we are content with what we have, we won't even think about taking something that doesn't belong to us.

If you take something that belongs to someone else, it is like taking something that belongs to God because He has given us all things—they are His too. We would never want to take something that belongs to God, would we?

It makes God sad when we take things that are not ours and it makes those we take the things from sad as well. God sees all things, and if you take something from someone else, God knows, even if they don't.

We are to do unto others as we would have them do unto us. Be content with the things that God has given you. We are all so very blessed.

Enjoy what you have and respect those things of others. It's the right thing to do.

Dear God,

Thank you for all the wonderful blessings You have given us. You have given us so much. Help us to be satisfied with what we have and to respect the property of others.

Day 11

"I can think about my future and plan the wonderful things I want to do when I grow up. God has a plan for my life."

Someone once illustrated our Thought for the Day in the following way: "Let's say we have an empty box. Let's give this box a job. We can stand it up on its side and pretend that it is a refrigerator! But wait…if we really use it for that, then all the food we put in it will begin to spoil. That won't work.

Ok, so we lay it flat, climb in it and use it for a car! But wait…we're too big to fit in the box. We'd crush it! Besides, it has no wheels…we wouldn't get very far.

Maybe we can use it for a hat! But wait…the box is too big for our head, and it really isn't very pretty. Hmmm…maybe this box just doesn't have a job, or a purpose.

But the box has to have a purpose. It was made for something! You can put things in the box and store things in it! That is what the box was made for! It is only really of value to us if we can use it for what it was made for" *(Kids of Integrity).*

This is a very good illustration, isn't it? The box is a lot like us. God says in Jeremiah 29:11, "For I know the plans I have for you…" God has a plan for our lives. He has a job just for us. He has a very important plan for each of us, and He wants us to find it and fulfill it…all with His help, of course!!

When you discover what God's plans are for you, you will find great joy in being what God made you to be. We look forward to seeing the plans God has for each one of you.

Dear God,

We thank You that You have a plan for our lives. We want to fulfill Your purpose for us.

Day 12

"I feel successful when I try. I will work hard and not give up."

How do you feel sometimes when something is rather hard for you to do? Do you sometimes just not want to even try to do it? That's the easy way out, isn't it? If you don't even try, you won't have to be bothered with it. But if you don't try, you won't know if you can do it and you just might be successful at what seemed so hard for you.

Trying to do things is the first step to being successful. If you don't ***try***, you will never ***accomplish*** anything. The important thing to remember is that if you try and don't get it right at first, keep trying. Don't give up!

You have to make up your mind to try and try again! You need to hang in there until you complete the task you started. You need to keep working at it, even if you run into problems in completing it. You need to keep on trying!

A man named Napoleon Hill said, "Edison failed 10,000 times before he made the electric light. Do not be discouraged if you fail a few times."

So, be successful by, first of all, trying, and secondly, by staying with it. Don't give up!

Dear God,

Help us not to give up when things are difficult for us, but to try and keep trying. We know that You help us through everything and we thank You for that.

Day 13

"Many hands make light work."

Do you know what that means? It means that when you share, help, or cooperate with others, you can accomplish a great deal more.

If you think about it, it really is very simple. The more persons working on something, the easier the job is.

For example, if there is only one person building a house, it is going to take a long time to get that house finished. However, if you have ten people building the house, working together, the job is much easier and it will take a lot less time for it to be completed.

Now how does that relate to you? Well, if you see someone trying to do something, why not pitch in and help them? It will make it much easier for them and the job will be completed much faster.

If your class is doing something together, do your part to help. It will get done faster and then maybe you will be able to do something even more fun.

Remember, "Many hands make light work", and the fact that you are doing your part in helping and cooperating makes the Lord happy as well. That all makes for a great day!

Dear God,

Please help us to do our part to cooperate with those around us, and to do our share of the work when there are things to be done.

Day 14

"Education is the most powerful weapon which you can use to change the world."

—Nelson Mandela

You know, when you come to school each day, you are being educated, aren't you? You are here to learn. It is amazing to see how much you learn from year to year.

Education and learning are two of the most important factors in becoming all that you can be. If you are willing to learn, this will help you be the best you can be in life.

One important thing to remember, however, is that you learn wherever you are, not just at school. Education is not just about studying subjects such as reading, science or history. Learning happens all the time. Anytime you are willing to learn, you can learn. Learning takes place throughout the day, in any situation ***if*** you are willing to learn.

Through people learning, the world has been changed for the better. It is unbelievable how many wonderful things have been created for us to use, just because someone learned something from each mistake that was made, or from just being open to learning.

Learning can sometimes be hard, but it can also be one of the most satisfying things we will ever do. Learning can help us change the world! So, today, enjoy learning!!! Take it all in! The results will be great. Wait and see!

Dear God,

Help us to enjoy learning and to take advantage of all that the teachers share with us each day. Help us to open our minds and to work to be the best we can be.

Day 15

"Think before you speak. Use your words to build others up, not tear them down."
—Proverbs 12

Proverbs 12:8 says: "The words of the reckless pierce like swords, but the tongue of the wise brings healing." You know, this simply means that our words have the ability to either build up or tear down those around us. We can destroy friendships instantly with a few words. However, we can also use our words to completely turn around someone's day and make it better.

Referring to our verse, we use reckless words when we just say something without thinking about how it may make the other person feel. When we speak before we think, our words can hurt deeply. We need to stop and put the other person before ourselves. When we do that, then we speak wisely.

In the same way, our words can be a powerful tool in helping others who are struggling with different things. Someone may be having a terrible day, but the words we speak can lift them up and help them feel hope. Our words can have a powerful healing effect.

So, think before you speak so that you don't say something that you may regret later. Look for opportunities to make someone else's day better by using your words to build them up.

You will have a better day by guarding your words before they come out of your mouth. Speak words that God would be pleased with.

Dear God,

Help us today to guard our tongues and speak only those things that will build others up, not tear them down.

Keep our hearts pure and ready to do what You would have us do and to speak what You would have us speak.

Day 16

"I find good in every person."

Do you do that? Do you look at each person you come in contact with and look for the good in them? Sometimes that's hard for us to do, isn't it? Sometimes if someone is a lot different from us, we have a hard time finding their good qualities because they may not like the same things we do. They may think differently from us and be a completely different person. Sometimes we don't even try to find the good things in people.

You know, each person was created by God and God gave each person good qualities. They may be different from yours, but God gave them to that person and that makes them special.

We all need to look for the good things in others because everyone has those good things in them that only God gave them. If you make a point of looking for those good things in others, you may be pleasantly surprised at how many friends you may end up with.

Listen to this short poem:

God makes each one of us, Special in every way. We need to look for the good things in others, Each and every day. We need to look beyond our differences, To see those strengths God gives, And, who knows, we may find, A new friend who lives within. (Author Unknown)

Dear God,

Help us to look for the good in others. Help us to realize that each person is special because You have created each of us in a special way.

Day 17
Easter

"He is alive!"

As you know, tomorrow is Good Friday and Sunday is Easter Sunday. It is good for all of us to think about what Easter is.

As you already know, Jesus died on the cross for our sins. He laid down His life to pay for our sins. Sins are when we do something on purpose that we know is wrong. A sin isn't the same thing as a mistake or an "oops".

On the same day that Jesus died, His friends buried Him in a tomb. Jesus' tomb was probably like a little cave in a hill with a big rock rolled in front of it.

After Jesus died, all the people who knew and loved Him were very sad. Just like we are sad if someone we know and love dies.

But on the third day after He died, Jesus rose from the dead. What does that mean? It means that Jesus wasn't dead anymore! It means that Jesus was not in the tomb anymore!

Jesus had risen from the dead! He was alive forever! Everyone who knew and loved Jesus was glad.

We are glad too, aren't we? Because He rose from the dead, we can live with Him forever!

So during this Easter season, remember what a wonderful thing God did for all of us! He is alive, and because of that, we can live with Him forever! How blessed we are!

Dear God,

Thank you for sending Your Son to die on the cross for us. Because of that, we have eternal life! What a gift you have given us! Thank you, Lord.

Day 18

"I think for myself. I know that in every situation I have a choice. I know that smart choices are choices that are good for me; choices that do not hurt anyone else."

Some decisions you make aren't terribly important. For example, you might decide to have chocolate ice cream instead of vanilla. However, other decisions may involve a choice between right and wrong, and it is, at that moment, that you must think for yourself and do the right thing.

Sometimes you may have to stop and think about what the right thing is, especially if some of your friends are trying to get you to do something you aren't sure about. You must learn to think for yourself.

Someone once published the following list of questions. These are questions that you need to ask yourself when trying to determine whether you should or should not do something:

- "What does my conscience (that 'little voice' inside my head) say about it?

- Could it hurt anyone—including me?
- Is it fair?
- How would I feel if this were done to me?" *(Sermons4Kids.com)*

The most important thing you can do is pray that God will give you the strength and wisdom to stand up for the right thing. Think for yourself, seek God's help, ask yourself questions to help you determine what is right and what is wrong, and then do the right thing and make God proud.

Dear God,

We pray that we will always strive to think for ourselves and do the right thing. Help us not to give in to what others might want us to do, but to do what You would have us do always.

Day 19

"When I do what I say I will do, I am being responsible."

When we tell someone we are going to do something and then follow through with it, we are showing them that we can be trusted to keep our word. We are being responsible.

The following is an example of being responsible:

A school principal looked around her school right before school started and saw so many things that needed to get done before the students arrived. She started to get very stressed because she knew she couldn't accomplish everything by herself.

One morning a group of parents, teachers, and other volunteers arrived at her office and told her that they had plans to come on a particular day and work together to get the building ready for the first day of school. She was thrilled to hear this.

A few days later, they did exactly what they had told the principal they were going to do. They worked together for an entire day and the building was absolutely spotless and ready for the students when they finished.

These people were not only being responsible, but such a blessing. The principal so appreciated them doing what they said they would do. Everyone benefited from them being so responsible and dependable.

Remember to always do what you say you are going to do so people will know you as a responsible person. You will be glad you did.

Dear God,

Help us to be responsible people, always doing what we say we are going to do.

Day 20

"I know what good attention is and what bad attention is. I attract good attention by being kind, successful, friendly, supportive, and happy. This is the kind of attention I want to attract."

You know, attention means "*taking notice*" of someone or something. Attract means "*doing something to cause someone to take notice*". So if we want attention from others, it should be because we are doing the things we should be doing.

One elementary school once started, what they called, an All-Star Program. Each week, during chapel, one student would be recognized for something good, kind, or thoughtful that a teacher had seen them doing during the week. This program is a very special example of how we can attract attention because of the good things we are doing. The students in this program were recognized for all kinds of wonderful things they were doing. Because of this program, students looked for ways to be kind and thoughtful to one another.

Isn't this the kind of attention that we want to receive? Of course, we don't want to do this just to attract attention. We want to do it because it's what God wants us to do.

Isn't this so much better than attracting bad attention because you are talking while your teacher is teaching the lesson? Or getting out of your seat without permission and your teacher calls attention to your misbehavior?

We want good attention. If you each had this All-Star Program in your school, there is no doubt that there would be many All-Stars who are doing the right thing. Concentrate on good attention! Attract good attention!

Dear God,

Help us to focus on attracting attention for the good things in our hearts and in our actions

MAY

Day 1

"I think for myself. I know that in every situation I have a choice. I know that smart choices are choices that are good for me; that do not hurt anyone, including myself."

Have you ever been with a group of your friends and they, as a group, decide they want to do something that you know is not exactly the right thing to do, but you go along with them anyway? What happens? You all get in trouble, right?

That's what happens sometimes, isn't it? We go along with the crowd and then we do what we know we shouldn't be doing. That's when we need to stop and think for ourselves.

If we don't feel right about what they have decided to do, that's when we need to stop and say, "What is the right thing to do?" We don't ever need to "go along" with the crowd. That's when people really start getting in trouble.

The older you get, the more of an issue this will become. Fifth graders, you are soon going to be in middle school. This school year is almost over. This is very important for you to remember. You need to start thinking for yourself now. You need to start getting in the habit of doing what you know is right, no matter what anyone else wants to do.

Think for yourself and be a good example. Who knows, if someone else sees you making a different choice, you may influence them to follow you and you might save them from doing the wrong thing as well.

Think for yourself. Make the right choice—the smart choice.

Dear God,

Help us to focus on thinking for ourselves and making the right choices, no matter how pressured we may be to give in to others. Strengthen us to make the right choices always!

Day 2

"Beauty on the outside is not near as important as being beautiful on the inside."

You know, we are not the way we look. Our looks do not make us who we are. Our looks are just external, or on the outside.

If we have true beauty on the inside, we feel good, and that makes us even more beautiful, or handsome, on the outside. People can quickly see our internal beauty, just by the way we act, and that, of course, reflects our outward beauty.

The spirit of the Lord—His loving-kindness—can create in us an inner beauty that far surpasses our external looks. If we have God's love in our hearts, that is going to be obvious to those we come in contact with. This, in turn, is going to show a great outward beauty to those who see it.

How much more important it is to be beautiful inside first—because if we have inner beauty, we will automatically be beautiful, or handsome, on the outside. Isn't that what we should want?

So, we all need to work on that inner beauty—being more Christ-like and doing what He would have us do. If we do that, then people will automatically see all that beauty extending outward.

Dear God,

Help us to be more concerned about our inner beauty rather than our outward looks. Help us to strive to acquire Your Christ-like spirit so that our inner beauty will extend outward.

Day 3

"I know that there are many ways to do one thing. I accept that not all people think the same and that not everyone thinks my way is best. It is okay for people to think differently."

You know, there are people who have grown up thinking that if people don't do things the way they do it, or the way their family does it, then they are doing it wrong. However, if you really think about that, there is something wrong with this idea.

Just because someone else doesn't do a job the way you go about doing it, it doesn't mean that they are doing it wrong. They are just doing it a different way.

As we have said before, God has given us all different abilities so we probably approach a job in different ways because we all have strengths in different areas. That's not a bad thing either.

Don't be so quick to judge someone who does something in a different way. The finished product is what matters. If the result is a good one, it doesn't matter how a person goes about doing it.

After all, there is a lot of variety in this world. Lots of people work toward the same goal, and have many different methods of accomplishing the goal. All are good.

Dear God,

Thank you for making each of us so uniquely different. Thank you for our abilities to accomplish the task ahead of us. Help us to see that there are many ways to do different jobs and that our way is not the only way to do it. Help us to see outside ourselves.

Day 4

"Others look at what I say and the way I say it to decide what they think about me. I will be mindful of what I say and how I say it."

We need to watch what we say so we don't sin with our tongue. We do that by being aware of what we say and how we say it, and learning to control our tongue.

Did you know that you can sin with your tongue? There are many, many ways that we can use our tongues to sin. Our words can either bless others or be the source of a lot of problems.

The Bible has a lot to say about our words. As Christians, our desire is to become more and more like Jesus. Part of that is learning how to speak the way He would speak.

The Bible tells us that the tongue is very powerful and hard to control. If we let Him, though, Jesus will help us to watch what we say and use our words to encourage and help others.

Help me to use my tongue, oh Lord, To make someone's day. Help me to guard my speech, And be careful of what I say. Help me to remember the power I have in my tongue. Make me aware of how I speak, And work on it while I'm young. Help me do all things according to Your will, And guard my words, my speech, and my actions, Seeking Your face in all things—quietly and still. (Author Unknown)

Dear God,

We know that our tongue is a powerful thing. Help us to guard the things we say carefully so that we will not hurt others or discourage those that we are speaking with. Help us to be aware that we are Your representatives and that You hold us responsible for each thing we say and how we say it.

Day 5

"What you do speaks so loud that I cannot hear what you say."
—Ralph Waldo Emerson

Another way to put our Thought for the Day is, "Actions speak louder than words." What you ***do*** shows others how you really feel and what you really believe. Someone once illustrated it this way: "What if I say my favorite color is red, but everything I own is blue? What if I say I eat only healthy food, but every time you see me, I'm drinking soda and eating potato chips? And how about if I say I'm your friend, but I ignore you when you talk to me? You would know that I don't really mean what I say" *(Kidsundayschoolplace).*

In the same way, some people say they love God, but they never obey His commands. Others may go to church and look really good on the outside, but in their heart they have a bad attitude, they get mad easily, or they disobey those in authority.

God cares about what you say ***and*** what you do. He cares about your actions and your inner attitude. If you really love God, it will show on the outside. God sees your heart as well. He knows if you truly love Him. So love God, not only by what you say, but by what you do.

Remember, your actions are much louder than your words!

Dear God,

Help us to act on what we say we believe. Help us to be doers of Your word and not hearers only. When we see a need, help us to step up to help. Give us the right attitude always, and help us be the best examples for You that we can be.

Day 6

"Working hard honors God."

Do you know what the Bible says about work? You know, our work matters to God. Working hard, no matter what you are working on, honors God. Colossians 3:23 says, "Whatever you do, work at it with all your heart, as working for the Lord, not for men."

So, whether you are doing your school work in class or at home, or whether you are helping your mom or dad, or whatever work you are doing, God expects you to do your very best.

The Bible talks about those who are lazy as well—those who don't do what God expects them to do, the way He expects them to do it. He does not look at them in a good way. He expects ***everyone*** to work with their whole heart—as if we're working for Him (because really we are).

So, today, whatever you have before you to do, do it with your whole heart, to the best of your ability. You are working for the Lord.

Dear God,

Thank You for giving us the ability to work. Help us to realize that we need to work for You. We need to do the best we can do in whatever we do, as unto You.

Day 7

"With God's help, I can be successful. I will be successful by doing the very best I can do and being the very best I can be."

What does it mean to be a success? Here's a clever poem which explains success:

> *Success isn't having trophies or toys, It isn't a medal or friends of your choice. What is success? That's easy to see. It's trying to be the best you can be! You don't need to worry about what others, May have or what they might say. When trying your best, Success comes your way. (Author Unknown)*

Of course, we have a part to play in making sure we are successful. Did you hear the part about being the best ***you*** can be? How do we do that? We work hard and do the best we can do in everything we do, as we read yesterday in our previous Thought for the Day.

Why should we always do the best we can do? Because that's what the Lord expects of us. Our God expects us to do our best at everything. This, in turn, will help us be successful.

Dear God,

Help us put our best foot forward and work on everything in front of us to the very best of our ability. Help us to expect the best from ourselves and push ourselves to give our best. We know that this is what pleases You.

Day 8

*"**No** God, **no** peace. **Know** God, **know** peace."*

The first phrase, "***no*** God, ***no*** peace" means simply that if we don't have God in our lives, we will have no peace or calm in our hearts. The second phrase, "***know*** God, ***know*** peace" means that if we know, or have a relationship with God, we know peace—we have peace in our hearts because we know He is taking care of our problems. He is helping us daily to get through those things that trouble us.

What do you think of when you think of peace? It means having calmness in your heart—even in the middle of a difficult situation. True peace only comes from God.

Even in the middle of a hard time, you can still have peace. That's a wonderful thing to know, isn't it? And it is all because of God.

If we love God, we will have great peace. We will have peace if we keep our mind on the Lord, not on ourselves.

The peace of God is greater than we can understand, but if we give our cares to Him, He will give us that peace even though we don't understand it. We will feel that calmness that comes from God. When we say, "God take care of this because I can't", He will—that's the peace that comes from the Lord.

Aren't we blessed to have a God who takes care of us and provides us the peace and calm that can't be understood? We are truly blessed to ***know*** God and to ***know*** peace.

Dear God,

Thank you for giving us that peace that transcends all understanding. Thank you for allowing us to give You all of our cares and troubles and know that You are helping us with those.

Day 9

"I will be grateful for all of the wonderful blessings that the Lord has given me."

Blessings are all the good things that we have been given by the Lord. The Lord, as our heavenly Father, gives us blessings everyday. He gives us sunshine, our families, our food and many other things. Think about all of the blessings that the Lord has given you today.

He has blessed you by waking you up this morning in good health, able to come to school. He has given you your family, and wonderful teachers who lovingly teach you each day. There are so many things He has blessed you with.

The blessing that the Lord wants to give us more than anything else, however, is the gift of a happy life in heaven forever. We need to strive daily to be a good example for others, and to do what the Lord wants us to do so we can have this ultimate blessing of eternal life.

So remember that the Lord loves to bless us. However, we need to be grateful for all He has blessed us with and never take it for granted. Listen to this poem about blessings:

Thank you, God, for my many blessings. Help me to be thankful everyday. Show me ways to bless others, So I can lead others in Your way. Daily help me see the treasures, You have put right before my eyes, So that I will remember, The God who gave them is the One most high.

May I show gratitude to the one Lord, my God, For each blessing I do not deserve, Giving all honor and glory, To our God whom we serve. (Author Unknown)

Dear God,

Help us to be grateful to You for all of our many blessings because we know that You don't ***have*** to give them to us. You ***want*** to bless us. Help us to have a grateful spirit.

Day 10

"We need to communicate with God each day through prayer."

What does it mean to communicate with someone? It means to talk with them. People communicate with others by talking face to face, talking on the phone, using their cell phones to text someone, sending e-mails, or by writing a letter to someone. There are lots of ways to communicate or talk with others.

How do we communicate or talk to God? Our Thought for the Day tells us. We talk to God through prayer. Prayer is communicating or talking with God. We may not be able to call God on the phone or send Him a letter, but prayer is just as real as any other form of communication.

Why should we pray? Because it makes our relationship with God stronger.

Can you imagine trying to have a best friend without communicating with them? Prayer is seeking God and His direction for our lives. Praying also keeps us out of trouble. Jesus told us to pray.

So, why pray? It's simple. To talk to God and to get His direction for our lives. God is so good and will help us when we are happy, sad, sick, or even when we're in trouble. God will give us wisdom, strength, and understanding if we only ask Him. When we pray, our relationship with God grows.

Dear God,

Thank You for being our God and for wanting to have a relationship with us. Help us to grow in You, Lord, by praying daily and asking for Your guidance. Help us to seek your help through prayer and to be guided by Your wisdom.

Day 11

"I treat others the way I want them to treat me. If I want people to help me, I help others. If I want them to encourage me, I encourage others. If I want them to love me, I love others."

You know, Luke 6:31 says, "Do unto others as you would have them do unto you." I bet if all of us stopped to remember this verse throughout the day, things would be a lot different, wouldn't they?

If every person consciously treated others the way they would want to be treated, this whole world would be a different place. What a wonderful world we would have to live in.

But that's what we, as God's children, are supposed to do. If we stop and think about how we would want others to treat ***us*** and then we treat ***them*** this way—Wow!—What a difference that could make!

So let's all try this today—as you go through your day—stop and think how you would like to be treated in each situation you find yourself in. Then treat your friends that way. What a great day I bet you will have!"

Dear God,

Help us to stop and remember to treat others the way we would want to be treated today. Give us the courage to do the right thing.

Day 12

"The secret to enjoying life is to be thankful for the people in your life and for what each day brings."

There are two little words in our English language that, perhaps, mean more than all others. They are "thank you"—being thankful for the wonderful blessings which are ours. When each day begins, we should be thankful for all we have been given; as each day progresses, we should be thankful for all we have been given; and when each day ends, we should be thankful for all we have been given.

All that we have is a gift from the Heavenly Father. How can we show Him that we are thankful for all that we have?

Think of the people who have taught you, encouraged you, loved you, and who have made a positive difference in your life. Now think back. Have you told them you are grateful for them, and why? That is something we can, and should, do.

Likewise, we need to be thankful for what each day brings our way. Some things are good things and some are not so good, but God can take anything and turn it around for good.

So give thanks! We have so much! Don't ever take it for granted! God is so good to us!

Dear God,

Thank You for our many wonderful blessings. Thank You for the people You have placed in our lives. Help us to tell them how important they are to us. Help us to always look at each day and see it as a blessing, no matter what it brings.

Day 13

"I do not give up; I keep trying until I am successful."

You know, many times when we try to work on something and it doesn't go the way we want it to, we get discouraged and we have a tendency to want to stop trying to do it. Each of you, more than likely, has felt this way at one time or another.

But we learn from our mistakes, don't we? Sometimes when we mess up on something, if we look at what we did incorrectly, and make an effort to correct it, we actually learn how to do it better.

Students, do you remember when you first learned to ride a bicycle? Most of you did not get it right at the beginning, did you? However, you kept trying, didn't you? You kept trying because you really wanted to learn to ride that bicycle. Eventually, after several tries, you learned to ride that bike all by yourself.

It's that spirit of not giving up that helps one to succeed. You need to remember that just because you don't get something right the first time, doesn't mean you can never get it right. Stay focused on the task and keep trying. Listen to this poem—it's called *Never Give Up:*

Two steps forward, one step back, I have to stay focused and stay on track. Two steps forward, one step back, Now is not the time to slack. Two steps forward, one step back, Determination, never will I lack. Finally, I will make it to the top, Two steps forward...never going to stop! (likesuccess.com)

Dear God,

Give us a spirit to keep trying, even when things get difficult and we want to quit.

Day 14

"God can, and will, forgive our sins because of Jesus."

Many of our Thoughts for the Day have focused on God's love for us all the time. He loves us when we're happy or sad, and He loves us when we are good or bad. He loves us forever and ever. God loves us so much that He sent His son, Jesus, to us to provide forgiveness for all of our sins.

That is a strange word, "sin". We need to talk about what it means. As you know, we don't always do what is right. Sometimes we choose to do wrong things. That is sin. When we know what is right, but we choose to do what is wrong, that is sin. We've talked about this before in one of our other Thoughts for the Day.

Someone once illustrated our forgiveness this way: "We can't clean up our own sins, but God can, and will, forgive our sins because of Jesus. Jesus, the Son of God, came to earth and died for our sins on the cross, and because of what Jesus has done; we can be forgiven of all our sins. Because of Jesus and what He did for us, God can, and will, forgive our sins. When Jesus comes in, the sins go out! And then our lives are new and different because Jesus comes to live inside of us" *(Kids of Integrity).*

Even if we sin again (and we will), the sins don't get stuck inside. Once Jesus lives inside of us, the sins can't get back inside again. Only Jesus lives there.

God has forgiven our sins because of what Jesus has done. And He will never count these sins as ours again. When God looks at us now, He only sees Jesus in us." Isn't that wonderful?

Dear God,

Thank You for loving us. Thank You for sending Your son, Jesus. Thank You for forgiveness of sin through Him.

Day 15

"I will be a cooperative person."

What does it mean when you say that you are a cooperative person? It means you will work with others, in such a way, that you will accomplish something. A teacher once listed the following nine things you can do to assure that you are, indeed, a cooperative person:

1. Listen carefully to others and be sure that you understand what they are saying.
2. Share when you have something that others would like to have.
3. Take turns when there is something that nobody wants to do, or when more than one person wants to do the same thing.
4. When there are disagreements, try to see the other person's side.
5. Do your part the very best that you possibly can. This will inspire others to do the same.

6. Show appreciation to people for what they contribute.
7. Encourage people to do their best.
8. Make people feel needed. Working together is a lot more fun that way.
9. Don't leave anyone out. Everybody has something valuable to offer, and no one likes being left out.

If you try really hard to follow these nine things, you will not have a problem being a cooperative person. Why not try it today? I bet you will see that it works!!!

Dear God,

We want to do what You would have us do. Help us to strive to always be cooperative people. Help us to do the right thing and to work hard to set good examples for others.

"I will tell the truth. I will always strive to be honest."

What is honesty? If you are honest, then you are truthful. When people are honest, others know that they will not lie to them, they will not steal from them, or they will not do anything that would cause them to question their actions.

Honest people are still going to make mistakes. No one is perfect except God. However, when people are honest, they own up to their mistakes and accept the consequences of them. They don't pretend to be something they are not.

With honest people, "what you see is what you get". They are not trying to be someone they are not.

"Honesty is important because it builds trust. When people lie or cover up mistakes, others can't trust them. When people aren't honest with themselves, they pretend that something doesn't matter when it does, or they exaggerate to impress others" *(Talkingtreebooks.com).*

In summary, being honest means:

- You don't lie.
- You admit your mistakes.
- You can be trusted.
- You stand up for the right things.
- You live a life that God wants you to live.

We need to always strive to be honest people. We need to be people who can be trusted, and people that God will be happy with.

Dear God,

Help us to always be truthful and honest. Help us to live a life that You are happy with.

Day 17

"Sharing with others makes me feel good and makes others feel good too."

One day the principal was in the lunchroom at her school during the students' lunchtime. She watched as a young student gave out cookies to each of her fellow students. She smiled as the young lady so graciously shared what she had brought with her friends. Her smile got even bigger, however, when the student came up to her and offered her a cookie as well. Wow!! She was so excited! She wasn't just excited about getting to eat a delicious cookie, but she was excited about the fact that the student cared enough to share one with her.

On another day, the Principal was visiting a classroom at her school when she saw a young man who needed a particular color crayon to finish his picture. He didn't have the color so his classmate offered to let him borrow one of his. That small act blessed the Principal's heart. It showed how willing the student was to share what he had with others.

These two examples illustrate what is meant by our Thought for the Day. Sharing with others doesn't just make us feel good, but it makes others feel good as well. And it doesn't just bless us; it blesses the Lord also. As He sees His people doing the things He wants them to do, He is blessed.

So keep on doing all those wonderful things you are doing to share with others. We are proud of you!! God is too!!

Dear God,

Help us to continue to show Your love to others and to help them when we can. Help us to exhibit Your love and kindness always and to look for ways to share what we have with others.

Day 18

"When something goes wrong, instead of feeling bad about it, I concentrate on what I can do next time to make it better."

You know, whenever we go through our day, we are not going to always have everything happen just the way we want it to. Everyday, something happens in each of our lives that we wish hadn't happened. No one has a perfect day.

However, what says a lot about you is how you respond to things when they go wrong. Don't beat yourself up and feel bad when things go wrong. Instead, pray and focus on what you can learn from this, and how you can make it better the next time.

Some of the world's smartest people are that way because they learned from their mistakes. But realize, they ***learned*** from their mistakes. We must learn from our mistakes in order to do better in the future. So don't beat yourself up when things go wrong. Learn what happened to make them go wrong, and see what you can do better the next time. That's ***learning*** from your mistakes.

Listen to this poem by a lady named Judy Lalli:

Mistakes can be good, They can help you grow, They can show you what you need to know. So whenever you make a mistake, Just say: Now, I'll try another way.

Dear God,

Help us learn through our mistakes. Help us not to beat ourselves up, but to come to You in prayer and ask that we will use our mistakes as a learning tool.

Day 19

"I can love God back."

We talk often about the fact that God never changes and that He will forever love us. The Bible tells us over and over how much God loves us. God shows us, in many ways, that He loves us. Let's list some of the ways God shows us that He loves us:

- He knows us better than we know ourselves and cares about us.
- He gives us good homes and families who love us.
- He gives us food to eat, and clothes to wear.
- He gives us friends who support us and stay with us no matter what.
- He sent His son to this earth to die for our sins.

It is a wonderful thing to know that God loves us! Did you know that God wants us to love Him back? Jesus said that the greatest of all the commandments was for us to love God!

Just like we talk to others on a phone, we can talk to God, too. We talk to God through prayer. Prayer is just one way to express our love to God. There are other ways we can show God that we love Him also. We can read the Bible, go to church, obey our parents, respect others, and make the right choices. When we do what He wants us to, we love God back.

God loves us so much! Love God back!

Dear God,

Thank you for creating us and loving us so completely. Help us to draw closer to You each and everyday. Help us to love You back, Lord, and to strive to daily walk in Your ways, according to Your will.

Day 20
Memorial Day

"When your mouth is closed, your ears and eyes magically open wider."

Have you ever thought about that? What does that really mean? Does this really happen? No, it doesn't magically happen that your ears and eyes open wider, but when you stop and listen and quit talking, you see and hear things that you wouldn't have seen or heard if you had continued to talk.

This is a good point because it is very difficult to learn anything if you are always talking. Even though our eyes and ears don't magically open wider, we are much more focused on hearing others and seeing things that are going on around us if we will just close our mouth and listen.

We often hear the phrase, "Generally speaking, you aren't learning much if your mouth is moving." And this is totally the point of our Thought for the Day. Close your mouth more, open your eyes and ears more, and you will probably learn a whole lot more.

**As Memorial Day is coming up, today, we also want to take some time to think about all the wonderful men and women who have given so much in serving our country and in fighting for us. As we pray, let's remember this special group of people who so deserve our respect.*

Dear God,

Help us to be better listeners and to be more attentive to the needs of those around us. Also today, Lord, we remember all those special men and women who have, and who continue to, serve our country. Thank you for them and their continued service.

Day 21

"God never changes."

So many things in our lives change. People grow older, friends come and go, sometimes we move to another place, but no matter what else may change, God is good and He never changes. Hebrews 13:8 says, "Jesus Christ is the same yesterday, today, and forever."

You know, as we said, things change all around us all the time. Sometimes people change. Do you grow? Do you learn new things? These are changes. We don't look the same as we did when we were very young, and our looks will change as we get older too. These are all changes.

We don't always like change, do we? If you move somewhere new and have to go to a new school, that can sometimes be scary, or cause you to worry. But there is one thing we can always count on: God does ***not*** change! Isn't that wonderful? God does not change—ever!

God loves us with a love we cannot even imagine and that will never change! God will love us forever! That will never change! He loves us and nothing will ever separate us from that love! That will never change!

Sometimes we are so happy! Sometimes we are sad or mad. Sometimes we are scared. Sometimes we are angry. God loves us through it all; no matter what we are feeling. He never changes!

Isn't that good to know? Even if lots of things change around us, even if we change, God always loves us and God does ***not*** change.

Dear God,

Thank you for loving us with a love that never changes. How blessed we are to have You as our God.

Day 22

"I will always tell the truth because that is what God expects me to do."

Do you know who is called the "Father of Lies"? It is Satan who is given this name. That's a horrible name to have, isn't it? However, it is given to Satan because you can never believe or trust anything he puts in your head.

On the other hand, God only speaks truth. He cannot tell a lie. He speaks only what is righteous and good. God can always be trusted.

As we've discussed before, honest people can be trusted also. What about dishonest people? Of course not. However, even though we all know what God wants us to do, we must still decide for ourselves whether we will be one of those honest, trustworthy people. There will be many times in our lives when we will have to choose to be like our Heavenly Father who speaks only truth, or choose to honor Satan by lying.

Remember, some people will not always like it when we tell the truth, especially if we say things they don't want to hear. But it is important to tell the truth no matter what others want you to say. We make God very happy when we speak the truth.

Before we tell lies to get something we want, we must remember that lying will not please God or our parents. Nothing is worth losing the trust of those we care about, and disappointing God who loves us so much.

Choosing to lie makes a person miserable because when we lie, we live in fear, waiting to find out when the lie will be uncovered. Just tell the truth because that is what God expects of us.

Dear God,

Help us to be truthful people. Help us to always tell the truth, no matter what.

JUNE

Day 1

"So you see! There's no end to the things you might know, depending on how far beyond zebra you go!"
***On Beyond Zebra*—Dr. Seuss**

Now what in the world do you think that means? Depending on how far beyond zebra you go? That sounds crazy, doesn't it?

But let's think about what Dr. Seuss was meaning when he put this in his book. Well, what's the last letter of the alphabet? Of course, Z. And just as the letter Z is the ***last*** letter of the alphabet, "zebra" is one of the ***last animals*** listed in the dictionary (for those of you who know what a dictionary is today). He is saying if you go beyond the last letter Z and the last animal, zebra, there is no end to the things you can do.

In other words, if you believe in yourself and ask God to help you, there is no limit to what you can do. There's no end to the possibilities!!

We look forward to seeing what the Lord is going to do in each of your lives. There's no end to the things you might know!

Dear God,

Thank You, Lord, for being our God, and for creating us with talents and abilities that we are not even aware of until You make them known to us. We know You have a purpose for each of us. Please help us to strive to always do all that we can do to fulfill Your purpose for our lives.

Day 2

"You can't win unless you know how to lose."
—Kareem Abdul-Jabbar

What exactly does our Thought for the Day mean? Well, it essentially means that you must be able to accept losses and learn from them in order to be able to win later.

If you are a sore loser when you lose or mess up, chances are that you are not in the right frame of mind to learn anything from what you did wrong. And if you don't learn anything from what you did wrong, you probably stand a good chance of not winning the next time.

As you can see, your attitude means everything. The right attitude can set you up for success. The wrong attitude can set you up for failure. It's truly up to you.

So you can't win unless you know how to lose. Have the right attitude when you lose and chances are that you will come much closer to winning the next time.

Dear God,

Please help us to have the right attitude when things don't go the way we want them to. Help us to learn from our mistakes, and to have the spirit that You would have us have.

Day 3

"I know how to listen. When I listen, I show others that I care."

Sometimes we have a hard time listening to other people, don't we? But God wants each of us to be careful listeners. Has anybody ever gotten mad at you because you weren't listening to them? What happened? It probably didn't go well, did it? Well, turn that around. How did you feel when someone didn't listen to you? Not so good, uh?

What are some reasons people don't listen? Most of the time it is because they want to tell you all about them and not listen to you. God doesn't like that, does He? What's wrong with not listening when someone is talking to you? Very simply, it's rude and disrespectful to them.

If you don't listen to your friends, you create bad feelings between you and them. Always remember, there is a big difference between hearing and listening. All too often, you may hear what others say, but you haven't really listened to them. You must stop and truly understand what they are trying to tell you and then respond to them and try to encourage them.

These five rules have often been used to help with good listening skills:

1. "Look directly at the person who is talking. Don't be doing something else while they are talking to you. Look at them.
2. Listen to them and don't interrupt them. Really hear what they are saying.
3. Ask questions about what they are saying. Let them know that you have an interest in what they are telling you.
4. Encourage them to keep talking with you by nodding your head, saying something in regard to their topic of conversation.
5. Repeat what they are saying in your own words. That way, they will truly know you listened to them" *(goodcharacter.com).*

Be a good listener—show others that you care.

Dear God,

Help us to show others that we care about them by listening to what they have to say to us.

Day 4

"I will work really hard to be prepared for class each day so I can do my best work."

You know, this school year is almost over so you are probably saying, "Why do we need to talk about being prepared for class when we are almost finished?" Well, you can use this Thought for the Day to help prepare you for your next school year because this is an important thing to remember everyday, no matter what.

Now, what does it mean to be prepared for class? First of all, being prepared for class means you show up on time, you have all your materials, and you are attentive. Why is that so important?

It's important for you to be prepared for class because it keeps your class on schedule. It also gives you more time in class to read, finish your assignments or work on projects. Not only that, but it makes class less stressful, sets a good example for others, and it keeps you out of trouble.

Ok, now, let's talk specifically about ***how*** you can be prepared for class. A teacher once shared the following ways to be prepared for class:

1. Gather all necessary books, papers, homework, and pencils/crayons/or pens.
2. Be on time for class, sitting at your desk when class begins.
3. Present homework and assignments when the teacher asks for them.
4. Write down assignments and homework completely. Don't leave anything out.

Being prepared for class is essential to your academic success. We know that, for the most part, all of you work really hard to be prepared for class, but if, after hearing this, you realize you are not always prepared for class, get ready for next year and turn this around!

Dear God,

Help us to always be prepared for class and to be the good students You want us to be.

Day 5

"If I do not have anything good to say, I say nothing."

Our words have the ability to either build up or tear down those around us. We can destroy friendships that we have had for years instantly with a few words. We can also use our words to completely turn around someone's day, for the better.

Think about a time when someone said something that made you feel really good. What did they say? Now, think of a time when someone said something to you that did not make you feel good.

After thinking about the above, answer this question—do the words that you say matter? You already know the answer to that question. The words we say affect those around us greatly.

Let's say that someone wants to be a part of your group of friends and you tell them no. That's hurtful and it is not the right thing to do. How would you feel if they said that to you? Think about it.

What if you are arguing with someone and you say something that hurts the other person's feelings? What could you do in the situation to help to make sure that you don't say something that you will regret later? Well, you could walk away and talk to them later when you have calmed down.

Remember our Thought for the Day: "If I do not have anything good to say, I say nothing." Our words impact others greatly—use them for good.

Dear God,

Help us to watch our words and make sure that they build others up and not tear them down.

Day 6

"My parents love me always."

Isn't this a great thought? Your parents love you ***always***—not just when you are being good, not just when they feel like loving you—but they love you ***always***—no matter what.

You can get in trouble in school one day, but do they love you any less? ***No***—they may be disappointed in your behavior, but they don't love you any less. They love you no matter what—that's called unconditional love—there is nothing you can do that will make them not love you.

You know, there is someone else who loves you with an unconditional love—do you know who that is? Yes, God. God loves all of us just like your parents love you.

We are blessed to have parents who love us unconditionally, but even more so, we are so blessed to have an awesome God who also loves us no matter what we do, even when we disappoint Him.

Love surrounds us every minute of the day! Praise God for that!

Dear God,

Help us to remember how loved we are. Thank You for our parents who love us so much and who sacrifice so much for us. We thank You for Your love as well. Even when we mess up, You still love us. Thank You, Lord, for that.

Day 7

"To have good friends, you must be a good friend."

Think of ways that good friends treat each other. There's no doubt that if you think long and hard, you can come up with a long list of positive things that make a person a good friend.

GoodCharacter.com published the following list to show the qualities of a good friend:

- "Good friends listen to each other.
- Good friends don't put each other down or hurt each other's feelings.
- Good friends try to understand each other's feelings and moods.
- Good friends help each other solve problems.
- Good friends give each other compliments.
- Good friends can disagree without hurting each other.
- Good friends are dependable.
- Good friends respect each other.
- Good friends are trustworthy.
- Good friends care about each other."

Now, if you were to make your own list of good friend qualities, would it be like this one? Surely it would be. We all know that these are the qualities that make a friend a good friend.

Don't forget how important it is to be a good friend to those around you. Friendship is very important. Be a ***good*** friend.

Dear God,

Thank you for the people that You have placed in our lives to be our friends. Help us to do what we need to do to be the best friend to them that we can be.

Day 8

"I will show respect to all those I come in contact with. I will honor others the way I would want them to honor me."

The word, respect, means "being concerned about the feelings, wishes, or rights of others." So if your teacher, or another authority figure, asks you to do something, you don't argue with them, or resist doing it, you say, "Yes Ma'am/Sir" and do it!

That's respect. That's what all of us expect here in our school. That's what God expects too.

Let's go through some other ways that you can be respectful:

- Always be nice to other people. Stop and think about how you would want them to treat you, and treat them the same way. If all of us did that each day, there would probably never be a problem with respect.
- Listen to others. Care enough about those around you that you really listen to what they have to say.
- Never act ugly to others by making fun of them, calling them names, or saying mean things to them.
- Never bully, or pick on anyone.

If we all worked really hard to do each of these things, respecting others wouldn't be a problem. Be respectful to everyone you come in contact with. It's what God expects of us.

Dear God,

Help us be respectful people. Help us to show honor to those we come in contact with and, in turn, show You honor because we know that this is what You want us to do.

Day 9

"I will not make fun of other people because that is not the right thing to do."

Have you ever seen someone make fun of someone else? Maybe you, yourself, have been a part of making fun of someone. You already know that this is not the right thing to do. And if ***you*** have done that, chances are that you didn't like yourself very much after doing it. You had to know that God wasn't very happy with you either.

Sometimes we start out just trying to be funny and then it gets out-of-hand. And as you know, we end up hurting others' feelings.

When you find yourself in these situations, and before you go too far, stop and think and ask yourself some questions:

- Would I want someone to treat me the way I am treating them?
- Is what I am doing hurtful to the other person?
- Are my words making that other person feel like he/she isn't as good as others?

- Is God pleased with my words? Do they build others up or tear others down?

Recently we talked about "If you can't say something nice about a person, don't say anything at all." We would all be better off if we stopped to remember this before we use our words to tear others down. Don't ever make fun of other people. God is not happy when we do this.

Dear God,

Help us to build others up with our words and actions, not tear others down. Help us to stop and think before we speak and act.

Day 10

"Good friends are like stars...you don't always see them, but you know they are always there."

Everyone needs friends. We often see the love that God has for us through the love of a friend. If you have a good friend, you surely know that there is a reason you were drawn to that friend. Our good friends have certain qualities that make us connect with them. Just as our Thought for the Day says, they are just like stars, shining bright and always there.

What makes a good friend? "First, good friends are always there for us, no matter what. Even if they live far away from us, they are still there for us. We always have a connection, no matter the distance. Our good friends love us no matter what.

Second, our good friends do not talk about us behind our backs. They are totally loyal.

Third, good friends are always available. If we need help, and they can help us, they do.

Fourth, good friends see our weaknesses and they forgive us. They realize that we are all human and mess up. Instead of turning their backs on us, they forgive us and we start again.

Fifth, good friends tell us the truth always. Even if it is something we don't want to hear, our good friends are truthful with us.

Lastly, good friends watch out for us. We 'have each other's back' so-to-speak. A good friend works to take care of us when we need support" *(Sermons4kids).*

So count it a privilege to be a good friend to someone else and to have good friends. They are shining stars, always ready to help us out. What a blessing!

Dear God,

Thank you for the blessing of friendship. Help us each to be a friend to others, and to look for ways that we can lighten others' burdens. Help us to never take our friends for granted.

Day 11

"Happiness is not brought about by what happens to us; it is brought about by what happens within us."

If we were to ask each of you to draw a huge smiley face on your paper and then list the things that the Bible says brings you happiness, what would you put there?

Would your list of things that the Bible says brings you happiness include a huge house, lots of money, and all the latest toys? Well, ***you*** may put those on your list, but you will not find that the Bible says those things bring you happiness. One reason for that is because they are ***things***.

Do you think that if you go through your day and nothing ever makes you sad, then this is what the Bible says brings you happiness? Again, the Bible does not say that this is happiness.

Well, what does the Bible say brings us happiness? Trusting in the Lord brings happiness.

There is a precious story that has been told many times to illustrate this point: "There once was a little puppy that noticed that whenever he was happy, his tail wagged, so he thought he had found the secret to happiness. One day he shared the secret to happiness with an older dog. He said, 'I have learned that happiness is in my tail. So I'm going to chase my tail, and when I catch it, I shall have happiness!' The old dog replied, 'I, too, believe that happiness is a marvelous thing for a dog and that happiness is in my tail. However, I have noticed that when I chase it, my tail keeps running away from me; but when I go about my business it follows me wherever I go' " *(Sermons4kids)*.

Don't be like the puppy chasing its tail. Remember, true happiness is trusting in the Lord. It follows you wherever you go.

Dear God,

Help us realize that our true happiness comes from knowing You and trusting You.

Day 12

"We should be thankful everyday in all situations."

First, and foremost, God's desire for everyone who believes in Jesus, is for them to be thankful. Through being thankful, we become closer to God, and feel His presence in our lives.

It is really easy to be thankful when we look at all the wonderful things that God has blessed us with. We are thankful for our wonderful friends, our teachers, our families, our homes, and the love that we share with all those so close to us.

But we don't always have wonderful things happen to us. We may be dealing with a medical issue, or there may be someone in our family who has died. There are all kinds of sad events that occur daily. It is very difficult for us to be thankful for those things. However, the Bible says to be thankful in ***all*** circumstances (or situations). How do we do that? Well, there are some things to remember to help us during these times.

Remember that God never changes. He is the same, no matter what. He loves you the same yesterday, today, and forever. You will always have Him right beside you no matter what.

Keep in mind that God's love is always there for you, and that even if your situation is not a good one, God is good. You always have God's listening ear when you pray to Him for help.

The Bible says that being thankful brings honor to God. Whether we see our situation as good or bad, we need to thank God because God can take bad things and turn them around for good. Be thankful always!! God is good!!

Dear God,

We have much to be thankful for. You have given us so many blessings. Help us never to take them for granted and to always give You credit for all the good that we have.

Day 13

"As I go into my summer vacation, I will continue to work, keep a good attitude, and look for ways to do good for others."

Today and tomorrow we will be talking about some things that are very important for you to remember this summer as you are enjoying a wonderful summer break.

First, we would remind you that just because it is summer, it does not mean that you stop working. We know that you won't have homework or school work, but try to stay busy. Help your mom and dad. Do chores and just help out where you can. You are generally happier if you have something to do.

Second, keep a good attitude. Your parents will probably ask you to do several things to help them since you will no longer be in school. Do it happily, with a good attitude, remembering how much they do for you.

Third, look for opportunities to do good for others. There are many people who just need someone to help them. Look for a chance to be a friend to another person and to help them out. Not only will this make them happy, it will make you happy as well.

Tomorrow we will talk about three other things you can do this summer to help yourself have a happier vacation. Your summer out-of-school can be much more than just time off. It can be a satisfying, beneficial time, not only for you, but for all those you come in contact with.

Dear God,

Direct our paths daily, not just during our time here at school, but during our summer vacation. Help us to hear Your voice as You guide us in the right way.

Day 14

"As I go into my summer vacation, I will remember the things I have learned this year, I will have fun, and I will thank God for the time I have to spend with my family and friends."

Yesterday we started talking about some things that are very important for all of you to remember this summer as you are enjoying your summer break. We talked about three things yesterday, and today we are going to talk about three more.

Our first reminder today is not to forget the things that you have learned this year—both in your studies and about God. You have learned so much and you have worked so hard. Remind yourself of those things. We realize you will be on break, but don't put out of your mind those things that are worth remembering.

Our second reminder is one that we probably don't have to remind you to do—have fun! Enjoy your time off! Appreciate all your family and friends. Don't forget how fortunate you are to have all those loved ones around you. Have fun!

Our third reminder, put a smile on your face and thank God that you have summer vacations and family and friends to enjoy them with.

Yes, this is our last day of school for this school year, but we will be praying for each of you and for your teachers this summer. You pray for them as well. You are never far from our thoughts. Have fun and remember how blessed you are to have all you have. Happy Summer Vacation!!

Dear God,

As we go into our summer break, help us to be happy and appreciative of all You have given us. Help us to stop and give You praise, honor and glory for all things. Please keep us all safe.

ABOUT THE AUTHOR

Joyce O'Bryant was raised in a Christian home in the mountains of Virginia. From there, she attended a Christian college where she met her husband of 41 years. She now lives in Hampton Roads, specifically, Yorktown, Virginia. She attends New Covenant Church in Hampton, Virginia.

While now retired, Joyce spent 25 years working in Christian education. She started by teaching 11th-12th grade college-prep writing, and later she progressed into the administrative field, working as both a high school and elementary school principal.

Always connecting closely with her students, on all levels, it was during her time at the elementary principal position that she felt the need to write daily thoughts to encourage her elementary students at the beginning of each day.

With her writing background and her interest in making a difference in young lives, she chose to make her daily thoughts into a book—*"Little" Thoughts for the Day.*

It is her desire that other administrators/teachers, and parents will use this book to encourage and inspire their students as well.

BIBLIOGRAPHY/REFERENCES

Credit is given to the following for the individual Thoughts:

1. "A Quotation-A-Day" Education World, June 6, 2002, accessed January 11, 2013. http://www.educationworld.com/a_lesson/lesson/lesson132.html.
2. Davies, Leah. "Character Building Thoughts for Children", accessed, December, 2012. http://www.kellybear.com/TeacherArticles/TeacherTip52.html.
3. "Positive Thoughts for Your Kids", accessed December 2013. http:///www.google.com/search?q=positive+thoughts+for+yourkids.

Credit is given to the three above websites for the "individual thoughts", however, the author has developed each thought independently herself. Credit has been attributed within the manuscript when material has been used from another source.

The author has not purposely taken anyone else's material without giving credit for it.

FOR THE DEVELOPING WORLD
LIBRARY
FOR ALL
DIGITAL LIBRARY

Printed in the USA
CPSIA information can be obtained
at www.ICGtesting.com
JSHW022324140824
68134JS00019B/1288

9 781683 508052